Praise for *Lincoln a*

"Rodrigue offers a concise yet nuanced ;
complex issues of how to restore peace
—*Journal of the Illinois State Historical Society*

"It is clear that Rodrigue has written a carefully researched, thoughtful, and valuable book that must be consulted by scholars in the future."
—**Paul Escott**, *Florida Historical Quarterly*

"Rodrigue takes the reader on a journey through Lincoln's presidency, highlighting critical moments that led the president to rethink how a war fought to restore the Union might actually be used to reconstruct a 'new nation . . . dedicated to the proposition that all men are created equal.' *Lincoln and Reconstruction* casts Lincoln as a leader willing to rethink his positions on matters of emancipation and racial equality but uncertain about how to adequately transform the postbellum South socially and economically. If Lincoln, as W. E. B. Du Bois once wrote, was 'big enough to be inconsistent,' Rodrigue's concise account helps us better understand how those inconsistencies reflected the president's political and intellectual evolution."
—**Keith Hébert**, *Civil War History*

"Readers interested in the Civil War era will likely find John C. Rodrigue's slim volume *Lincoln and Reconstruction* to be an intriguing study."
—***Southwestern Historical Quarterly***

"Lincoln's plan for reconstruction is generally shunted off to a single chapter or less in broader histories of the period. John Rodrigue gives the subject the full attention it deserves in this well-researched and carefully argued book."
—**James Oakes**, author of *Freedom National: The Destruction of Slavery in the United States*

"Rodrigue has provided a thoughtful, rewarding, and essential contribution to the study of reconstruction. With sharp analytical insight, he argues that Lincoln's role in defining reconstruction was fundamental to its goals and politics. This examination, with its compelling analysis and painstaking research, is certain to challenge our understanding of Lincoln's 'practical statesmanship.'"
—**Orville Vernon Burton**, author of *The Age of Lincoln*

"Sometimes a book comes along which analyzes and explains a difficult and complex subject in a clear, concise, and comprehensive manner. Such a book is *Lincoln and Reconstruction*. Though the president was murdered before the full unveiling of a reconstruction policy, the author, to his immense credit, does not rely on speculation and gives us Lincoln's actual thoughts and conduct that fairly describe his evolving views on the subject. To this author, Lincoln's leadership demonstrates that partisanship and political ruthlessness can be used to advance the highest ideals—reunion and freedom."

—**Frank J. Williams**, retired chief justice of the Rhode Island Supreme Court and founding chair of the Lincoln Forum

"All readers will gain fresh insights from Rodrigue's analysis of the enduring historical controversies over *Lincoln and Reconstruction*."

—**Joseph G. Dawson III**, Texas A&M University

CONCISE
LINCOLN
LIBRARY

—

EDITED BY RICHARD W. ETULAIN,
SARA VAUGHN GABBARD, AND
SYLVIA FRANK RODRIGUE

JOHN C. RODRIGUE

Lincoln and Reconstruction

Southern Illinois University Press
Carbondale

Southern Illinois University Press
www.siupress.com

25   24   23   22   4   3   2   1

The Concise Lincoln Library has been made possible
in part through a generous donation by the Leland E.
and LaRita R. Boren Trust.

Cover illustration adapted from a painting by Wendy
Allen

The Library of Congress has catalogued the 2013
hardcover and ebook editions as follows:
ISBN 978-0-8093-3253-3 (cloth)
ISBN 978-0-8093-3254-0 (ebook)

Library of Congress Cataloging-in-Publication Data
Names: Rodrigue, John C., author.
Title: Lincoln and reconstruction / John C. Rodrigue.
Identifiers: LCCN 2022029101 |
ISBN 9780809338917 (paperback)
Subjects: LCSH: Lincoln, Abraham, 1809–1865—
Political and social views. | United States—Politics
and government—1861–1865. | United States—
History—Civil War, 1861–1865—Economic aspects. |
United States—History—Civil War, 1861–1865—
Social aspects. | Reconstruction (U.S. history,
1865–1877) | Politics and war—United States—
History—19th century. | War and society—United
States—History—19th century. | BISAC: HISTORY /
United States / Civil War Period (1850–1877) | HISTORY
/ United States / 19th Century Classification: LCC
E458 .R64 2022 |
DDC 973.7—dc23/eng/20220722
LC record available at https://lccn.loc.gov/2022029101

SIU
Southern Illinois University System

To the memory of
Jackie (Rodrigue) Hafemeister

CONTENTS

Acknowledgments xi

Introduction 1

1. From Restoration to Emancipation
   (March 1861–January 1863) 14

2. From Emancipation to Reconstruction
   (January–December 1863) 44

3. War, Reconstruction, and Reelection
   (December 1863–November 1864) 75

4. "Into Proper Practical Relations with the Union"
   (November 1864–April 1865) 109

   Epilogue: What If 143

   Notes 151
   Bibliography 157
   Index 159

LINCOLN AND RECONSTRUCTION

INTRODUCTION

Although the name Abraham Lincoln is virtually synonymous with the American Civil War, it is less commonly associated with reconstruction, the period following the war when the nation faced the challenges of reintegrating the former Confederate states into the Union and addressing the consequences of emancipation.* Lincoln's assassination at the end of the war largely accounts for this discrepancy. Yet even in the recent historical literature that has viewed the Civil War as a period of revolutionary transformations in American life, with emancipation occupying a central place, scholars have tended to downplay Lincoln's role in inaugurating these changes. While there has been a notable literature on Lincoln's "wartime" reconstruction initiatives, the general consensus holds that they had made little headway by war's end. These efforts, moreover, are often seen as prologue to the story of postwar reconstruction, which witnessed the monumental battles between Andrew Johnson and congressional Republicans over policy toward the South, the former slaves' struggles to create a meaningful freedom, and the determination of white southerners to reestablish racial dominance.

---

* Throughout this book, "reconstruction" is rendered in lowercase. Although customarily capitalized, the term denotes a period of US history (1865–1877) that only assumed meaning after the Civil War. Also, because Lincoln and other contemporaries usually employed the lowercase, that practice is retained for the sake of consistency. The period following the war is generally referred to herein as "postwar reconstruction."

Lincoln's primary focus, in any event, was on winning the war; all other considerations remained secondary. Neither Lincoln nor Civil War–era scholars have ignored the topic of Lincoln and reconstruction, but they have generally relegated it to secondary importance.

Yet if Carl von Clausewitz's dictum that war is the continuation of politics by other means is valid, then the Civil War was essentially a problem of reconstruction. The eleven states that made up the Confederate States of America maintained that they had the right to secede from the Union and form their own nation—that their membership in the Union was voluntary and required the consent of the governed. Not only had the seceded states dissolved their relations with the United States and formed their own government, but, by raising armies and waging war, they had also undertaken the essential operations of an independent nation-state. Following the logic of Andrew Jackson during the nullification crisis of the early 1830s, Lincoln and most northerners countered that no state could leave the Union without the consent of the other states lest it compromise the integrity of the Union as a whole. In effect, the Union was permanent, secession illegal, and the Confederacy illegitimate. The Civil War thus involved suppressing an internal rebellion and restoring the seceded states to the United States. The war, in essence, was about a restoration—or "reconstruction"—of the Union.

This book provides an overview of Lincoln and reconstruction and proposes an alternative way of thinking about this topic. Traditionally, it is possible to identify two modes of thought on the scholarship on Lincoln and reconstruction. The first examines Lincoln's reconstruction policies in an attempt to discern what he might have done after the war had he not been assassinated, and therefore to speculate on how postwar reconstruction might have been different. Working within this "what would Lincoln have done" framework, scholars have offered differing interpretations on such questions as whether Lincoln was conservative or radical, whether he would have supported black civil rights, whether he would have imposed harsh terms on former Confederates, and the like. The second mode, by contrast, tends to view Lincoln's wartime reconstruction policies not as ends in themselves but rather as means toward the end of winning how Lincoln might have handled postwar reconstruction, the limits of his thinking would have been reached not on racial equality, which has received so much scholarly attention, but on the social and economic remaking of southern plantation society. By the end of the war, and in his famous "last speech," Lincoln had endorsed limited black suffrage, and it is not difficult to envision him eventually coming to embrace black suffrage in general, a nonracial conception of American citizenship, and the incorporation of African Americans into the nation's body politic. However, Lincoln was also a quintessentially centrist, mainstream Republican who adhered to the principle of absolute property rights grounded in a system of law. He was thus unlikely ever to have endorsed the kinds of measures—including land confiscation, which might have provided land to former slaves while breaking the power of the South's planter elite—that a genuine reconstruction of southern society would have required. In short, a postwar reconstruction under Lincoln would have foundered not on race but on economics.

Thus, Lincoln's reconstruction initiatives are best understood not as a means of winning the war but as ends themselves. Yet even as emancipation transformed the meaning of the war, for Lincoln and most northerners, so too was Lincoln's conception of reconstruction transformed—from the restoration of states to the remaking of southern society. Although, by the time of his death, Lincoln had only begun the process of seriously confronting the consequences of emancipation, he had already distanced himself from positions he had held at the start of the war. Nonetheless, Lincoln's wartime measures are not necessarily indicative of what he might have done after the war. Because Lincoln's conception of reconstruction changed so dramatically during the war, we can only speculate as to how far his thinking would have evolved once he confronted postwar circumstances.

If Lincoln's definition of reconstruction expanded to include transforming southern society, the war also became inseparable from the process of transformation. Lincoln always remained focused on military victory, but even before victory was assured, he could not avoid contemplating what the South and the nation would look like once the rebellion had been suppressed. Certain issues relating to reconstruction, which Lincoln would have preferred to postpone until the war's end, threatened the fragile political coalition essential to military victory. Lincoln therefore had to pursue, and balance, the two distinct but interrelated goals of Union and reconstruction. Simultaneously, although these two goals may have overlapped, Lincoln was compelled to consider them separately. War may well be politics by other means, but implementation of the political ends for which war is waged must customarily be postponed until military victory is secure. Those who wage war cannot afford the luxury of planning for the postwar world before they have achieved victory, yet neither can they afford to wait until military victory has been achieved before preparing for the postwar world. Thus, while Lincoln always insisted that everything he did was geared toward preserving the Union, a goal that ultimately hinged on military success, he also had to confront issues relating to reconstruction even when military victory seemed in doubt.

In addition to exploring how Lincoln's rethinking of the war and of the place of black people in American society shaped his evolving approach to reconstruction, this book addresses other factors that contributed to that evolution. It looks at events and developments in the seceded states where some form of wartime reconstruction took place—especially Louisiana, Tennessee, Virginia, and Arkansas—and shows how they both influenced and were influenced by events in Washington, DC. In particular, it examines how Lincoln attempted, by turns, to mediate, intervene in, or avoid altogether the intractable conflicts between conservative and radical Unionists and federal military and civilian authorities. It traces how Lincoln dealt with repeated calls from various northerners for negotiations with the Confederacy, and how his deflecting of those calls, especially from early 1863 on, became integral to his defense of emancipation as a war goal and as a condition of reconstruction. And it shows how tensions and conflicts between radical and moderate or conservative Republicans, especially in Congress, influenced Lincoln's handling of reconstruction. On the perennial question of whether relations between Lincoln and the Radical Republicans are better characterized by conflict or agreement, a question historians have debated for decades, this book tends to highlight the latter perspective. No claim is made to an exhaustive analysis of these topics; instead, they are examined in relation to Lincoln and reconstruction.

Because emancipation figures so prominently in the transformation of Lincoln's approach to reconstruction, it is necessary to understand how his views on slavery and race had evolved by the time he became president. This topic has generated some of the most contentious debate in all the scholarship on Lincoln. At one end of the spectrum are Lincoln's defenders, who virtually argue, as Eric Foner has observed in critiquing this position, that he was born pen-in-hand ready to sign the Emancipation Proclamation. All of Lincoln's earlier life, according to this view, becomes prologue to the fulfillment of his destiny as the Great Emancipator. At the other end are his detractors, who criticize Lincoln for embracing much of the racial prejudice endemic to nineteenth-century American society. This Lincoln did not lead the nation boldly toward emancipation but rather dragged his feet every step of the way. Evidence can be assembled to support either viewpoint. The solution to this apparent paradox rests not "somewhere in the middle" but rather in seeing Lincoln within his own historical context and not ours, and in recognizing both his limitations and his ability to reassess his own views.[2]

"I have always hated slavery, I think as much as any Abolitionist," Lincoln proclaimed in an 1858 speech. Yet he forthrightly added: "but I have always been quiet about it until this new era of the introduction of the Nebraska Bill began." Indeed, before the 1854 Kansas-Nebraska Act transformed the American political landscape, by revoking the prohibition against slavery in most of the Louisiana Purchase territory under the 1820 Missouri Compromise, Lincoln had devoted little thought to slavery or race. He instead tended to see them as distractions, deflecting attention from the Whig program of activist government in promoting economic development. Early in his political career, Lincoln had established himself as a moderate critic of slavery, occasionally taking public stances against it but also criticizing abolitionists whose tactics and zealotry he saw as a threat to the Union (though he also condemned the anti-abolitionist violence that spiked in the North during the 1830s). Neither had he been above employing racial demagoguery, though mild by the standards of the day, when politically useful. Of an essentially moderate temperament, Lincoln envisioned a gradual abolition of slavery, though readily confessing to having no idea how to achieve that end. "If all earthly power were given me," he admitted in his first major speech on the Kansas-Nebraska Act, "I should not know what to do, as to the existing institution." By the mid-1850s, Lincoln had formulated neither a coherent antislavery ideology nor a concrete political strategy for eliminating the institution. And while he, like many Americans, hoped for slavery's eventual extinction, he did not advocate racial equality and foresaw no meaningful place for free black people in American society.[3]

It is likewise axiomatic that while Lincoln personally detested slavery, he also believed—as did most Americans, including many abolitionists—that the federal government under the constitution was powerless to interfere with it in the states where it existed. He deemed the constitution neither a proslavery nor antislavery document but rather a compromise by its designers. The Founding Fathers, in his view, had generally believed slavery to be morally wrong but had implicitly sanctioned it out of necessity; they therefore tried to prevent its spread in hopes that future generations would find a way to eliminate it. Yet while the federal government could not interfere with slavery in the states, Lincoln believed that it undoubtedly possessed the power to regulate it in the territories. This regulatory power, moreover, did not include the discretion to prohibit, permit, or mandate the extension of slavery. Instead, slavery was so obviously wrong, and the Founding Fathers had so clearly meant to eradicate it, that for Lincoln regulation meant prohibiting its spread.

For Lincoln, however, something had gone wrong. In particular, the rise of an ideology deeming slavery a "positive good" (partly in reaction to abolitionist attacks) had replaced the revolutionary generation's "necessary evil" viewpoint. To be sure, slavery had steadily expanded ever since the United States gained formal independence in 1783, and its theoretical defense had become correspondingly more aggressive. Still, Kansas-Nebraska marked, as Lincoln had put it, a "new era." Under the principle of "popular sovereignty" (whereby the residents of a territory would decide whether to permit slavery), the federal government would now facilitate slavery's introduction into territory from which it had previously been "forever" prohibited. Lincoln's belief in the corrupting of an earlier antislavery consensus may have reflected a selective reading of American history, but this viewpoint enjoyed wide currency in the North. Thus, the principle underlying the Kansas-Nebraska Act had to be reversed in order to put slavery back on the path to ultimate extinction.

Kansas-Nebraska revitalized Lincoln's political career, which had been in abeyance since he left Congress five years earlier, and provided him the single idea—opposition to slavery's extension—that eventually gained him the presidency. During the second half of the 1850s, however, Lincoln faced the dual challenges of building a political coalition around this central idea while formulating an ideology that augmented the critique of slavery with a positive affirmation of the virtues of northern society. Essential to Lincoln's political genius was the ability to articulate commonly held ideas, and once he joined the Republican Party in 1856, after some hesitation over abandoning the Whigs, he made opposition to slavery extension the party's raison d'être, but he also helped to fashion its distinctive "free-labor" ideology. This outlook, which galvanized northern society before the Civil War, comprised a set of interlocking and mutually reinforcing ideas, values, and beliefs that espoused the North's superiority over southern slave society. The free-labor ideology affirmed the dignity and ennobling quality of manual labor, rejecting the South's equating of manual labor with slavery; it celebrated the openness and upward social mobility of northern society, in contrast to the South's rigid social hierarchy dominated by the planter elite; and it espoused the mutuality of interests between capital and labor, repudiating such notions as the inherently exploitative quality of capitalist relations and the immutable conflict between capital and labor. Formulated partly in response to the proslavery critique of industrial society and of "wage slavery," the free-labor ideology reflected a world of small, independent property holders, especially farmers and skilled craftsmen. Equally important was the idea that the South and its "positive-good" defense of slavery threatened everything northern society stood for. Thus, Kansas-Nebraska was but part of a coordinated campaign by the "slave power" to nationalize slavery.

Yet for all of Lincoln's hatred of slavery, he generally criticized it in moderate terms. Lincoln rarely dwelt on slavery's daily horrors, the abolitionists' stock-in-trade, and he refrained from condemning the slaveholders themselves. Slavery's greatest crime, for Lincoln, was that it systematically robbed the slaves of the fruits of their labor. It violated the essential truths that only labor truly created value and that all human beings would be motivated to work both to provide for their basic needs and to improve their quality of life. Slavery was part of what Lincoln called the "tyrannical principle" in his famous 1858 debates with Stephen A. Douglas: "It is the same spirit that says, 'You work and toil and earn bread, and I'll eat it.'" In distinguishing between the abolition of slavery and prohibiting slavery's extension into the territories (while also rejecting more aggressive uses of federal power to restrict extension, as some other Republicans advocated), and by linking the virtues of free-labor society to the economic robbery of slavery, Lincoln managed to situate himself by the latter 1850s at the center of northern antislavery politics.[4]

Just as Lincoln distinguished between slavery and its extension, he likewise emphasized the distinction between slavery and race, denying that the abolition of slavery would lead to racial equality. Lincoln occasionally pandered to racist sentiment, especially in countering the efforts of both abolitionists and Democrats—though for different reasons—to blur the distinction between slavery and race, and he explicitly opposed black suffrage and "social" equality. Lincoln's racism did not merely provide political cover for his antislavery principles, for in many respects it was genuine. And yet, he also insisted that the central principles of the Declaration of Independence—that "all men are created equal" and are endowed with the inalienable rights of "life, liberty, and the pursuit of happiness"—applied to black people. He rejected the assertion in the *Dred Scott* decision that black people could never become American citizens, and by offering an open-ended conception of American freedom, as an ideal to be aspired to, he allowed for a potentially broader definition of citizenship.

Lincoln did not obsess over race, as did many northerners, but he did not try to avoid it. To the contrary, he frequently addressed the issue during the latter 1850s and was compelled to do so repeatedly during the Lincoln-Douglas debates. Lincoln neither embraced nor condemned racism to the degree that he might have, and his outlook was perhaps shaped by an unfortunate deference to the will of the majority, whose views, however objectionable, must prevail in a democracy. Still, before the war Lincoln never thought of black people as essentially Americans, as being *of* as well as *in* American society. Nothing better reflected this outlook than his support for colonization—the idea of resettling former slaves and free black people, under government sponsorship, in Africa, the Caribbean, or Latin America. Lincoln saw colonization as integral to ridding the United States of slavery, not just before the war but well into it; and once the war commenced, colonization became central to his early approach to reconstruction. Lincoln's support of colonization may disappoint modern sensibilities, but it would also show how far he had moved on racial equality by the end of his life. [5]

Much of the commentary on Lincoln and race has tended to conflate two distinct but interrelated issues. The first concerns Lincoln's recognition of white racism as an objective fact, aside from his own personal views, and of the dim possibilities for black people ever achieving equality in American society. The second is whether Lincoln himself believed, even implicitly, black people to be inherently inferior to white people, and thus whether it was legitimate to subject them to legal discrimination, even though certain basic rights would be protected. Scholars sometimes collapse these two questions, such that on those occasions when Lincoln discussed white racism, even to deplore it, it has been attributed to him personally. Lincoln's objective recognition of white racism inevitably raises the difficult issue of whether he too willingly accommodated it—essentially washing his hands and declaring it to be a fact of life about which there was little anyone could do—or whether he could have taken a firmer stand against it. Yet even to the extent Lincoln believed black people to be inferior, at least before the war, there remains the question of whether he believed this supposed inferiority to be inherent or the result of conditions to which they had been subjected in America. Long before the advent of modern sociology and psychology, a strand of nineteenth-century racial thought held that black people's debasement should be viewed as the *result of* rather than as the *justification for* slavery and discrimination, a point of view with which Lincoln was familiar. Lincoln no doubt employed language and expressed views that reflected the racism of mid-nineteenth-century American society. Yet those views were sometimes expressed for political effect, were often descriptive rather than proscriptive, and signified what today might be described as "nurture over nature." Perhaps what was most important on the issue of Lincoln and race was Lincoln's ability to grow—to question his own views in light of new information and changing circumstances. Lincoln's racial views before the war would greatly evolve during it, along with so much else.

In the examination of Lincoln and reconstruction presented here, other important ideas must be taken into account. Lincoln once described reconstruction as "the greatest question ever presented to practical statesmanship," and it is perhaps fitting that this pragmatic statesman was adamant in seeing reconstruction as a practical rather than as a theoretical problem. Despite the beauty of his prose or the systematic quality of his mind, Lincoln was not a particularly abstract or original thinker. It is therefore somewhat paradoxical that his conceptualization of the war embraced the theory—or the "legal fiction"—that the seceded states had never left the Union. Lincoln had no choice in taking this view, for to do otherwise would have legitimized the Confederacy. Still, this perspective had important consequences, for it meant that certain policy positions regarding reconstruction necessarily followed from the very logic Lincoln applied to secession. Lincoln was not paralyzed by constitutional niceties, and on several occasions during the war he argued that actions that would not have been strictly constitutional in peacetime were necessary during a national emergency. And yet, for the purpose of suppressing the rebellion, Lincoln as commander-in-chief enjoyed vast powers under the constitution whereas on matters pertaining to reconstruction he had far less discretion. He could declare free, for example, the slaves in states engaged in rebellion, but he could not abolish slavery in those states nor define the rights of the former slaves. Although Lincoln considered the war and reconstruction inseparable, he could take certain actions on the former that on the latter he could not.[6]

Any analysis of Lincoln and reconstruction must also take into account Lincoln's untimely death. Historians' approach to Lincoln and reconstruction is almost entirely predicated on the knowledge of Lincoln's assassination. In some cases, it even seems as though Lincoln himself suspected during those "final weeks" that he would soon be removed from the historical scene. Yet this was obviously not the case. To the contrary, everything Lincoln did during his first term was undertaken with an eye toward the Union ultimately prevailing and with a general expectation that he would play a role in shaping the postwar settlement. Certainly, after his reelection in November 1864, he anticipated that his second term, which he had every expectation of fulfilling, would be dominated by reconstruction. Hindsight poses a problem in all historical analysis, but it particularly does so for Lincoln and reconstruction, since the sense of what-might-have-been has so infused this topic. Lincoln often commented on his own mortality, but he had no reason to think that the evening of April 14, 1865, would mark his last conscious moments on earth. Thus, it must be kept in mind that the way we view Lincoln and reconstruction was fundamentally different from the way Lincoln himself viewed reconstruction.

Finally, in examining Lincoln and reconstruction, this work focuses most of its attention on the thoughts, words, and, at times, actions of Lincoln himself. It has not attempted to incorporate systematically what Lincoln's many observers reported him as having said or done. Several such accounts, including those of John Hay, Frederick Douglass, and a few others, have been utilized when necessary. However, the focus is on Lincoln's own written and spoken words. Thus, while this work offers an overview of Lincoln's reconstruction initiatives, including how they unfolded in the seceded states, it can also be thought of as an extended essay on Lincoln's *thinking* on reconstruction. Although a politician and not a political philosopher, Lincoln nonetheless devoted much thought to this intractably practical problem.

FROM RESTORATION TO EMANCIPATION

(March 1861–January 1863)

The election of Abraham Lincoln as president in November 1860 precipitated the secession crisis, which culminated in Confederate forces firing on Fort Sumter on April 12, 1861, and in the fort's surrender the next day. Immediately following Lincoln's election, authorities in the eleven states that would form the Confederacy initiated the process by which their states seceded from the Union. South Carolina did so first, on December 20, and during the next several weeks, six more lower-South states followed suit, notwithstanding debate within each of them between advocates of immediate secession and those who encouraged the southern states to cooperate with each other before seceding. Although some outright opponents of secession joined the latter group, deliberations between "immediate secessionists" and "co-operationists" were largely over the method of seceding and not its legitimacy. Joining the seven states that had seceded by Lincoln's inauguration in March 1861 were the four upper-South states that seceded after the start of hostilities. While South Carolina's action ensured that the Union would undergo some kind of "reconstruction," the events of April removed any doubt.

Thus, Lincoln and most northerners originally went to war to restore the Union. However, just as a war for Union also became a war against slavery, a process of reconstruction initially limited to restoring the national authority over the seceded states was transformed into one in which those states faced the choice of submitting to that authority or seeing their slaves declared "forever free." Restoring the national authority always remained central to Lincoln's definition of reconstruction; and the Emancipation Proclamation, however revolutionary, was in many respects a narrowly conceived document. Yet by late 1862, the policy of emancipating slaves in the seceded states had become linked to the process of restoring the national authority over those states, even if the implications of that connection were entirely unclear.

I

As his inauguration approached, Lincoln's response to secession revealed a misunderstanding of the southern white mindset. He had said almost nothing during the presidential campaign, believing that he had already made his position on the slavery question abundantly clear in years of speeches and writings. Even as president-elect, Lincoln continued this silence, causing debate ever since over whether he should have more actively sought a compromise. Part of Lincoln's reasoning for keeping silent was the adverse effect any pronouncement might have on northern public opinion. But an equally important consideration was Lincoln's mistaken belief that secession was the work of a small minority that had managed to inflame the public mind. Co-operationists had run well in the seceded states during the election of delegates to secession conventions, and secession in the upper South had apparently stalled. A pronouncement now, Lincoln believed, might further stir things up. Given time, cooler heads would prevail, southern Unionism would assert itself, and the crisis would be averted. This had happened previously—in 1820, 1832, and 1850—and might happen again. Lincoln was hardly alone in overestimating Unionism and underestimating secessionism in the South, but his misreading of secessionist sentiment profoundly shaped his initial approach to reconstruction.

Even when Lincoln broke his silence, he wanted to see secession as a temporary crisis. In the dozens of speeches he gave during his well-publicized February trip from Springfield to Washington, he implored northerners to stand firm for the Union and make no compromises on slavery extension, but he repeatedly asked southerners what wrongs had they suffered from the federal government. Although events in the South seemed to indicate that war might well be unavoidable, Lincoln continued to hope that white southerners would come to their senses. As Harold Holzer has shown, some of Lincoln's remarks during the trip even suggest that he grossly underestimated the seriousness of the crisis, referring to it more than once as "artificial." Perhaps guilty of wishful thinking, he was confident that southern loyalists would take charge.[1]

Lincoln's speeches were designed to lay the groundwork for his inaugural address. Given all that had happened since the election, the inaugural had to incorporate two separate, almost contradictory, paths of reasoning. First, Lincoln argued that so long as war had not yet started, the situation could still be salvaged, and the states that had already seceded could resume their former relations. This line of thought might require changes to address the secessionists' complaints, for instance the proposed constitutional amendment that would have protected slavery in the states from federal interference, but it held that the "normal" state of affairs could still be restored. At the same time, Lincoln had to recognize that the nation was long on the way toward splitting apart. This line of thought would have to admit, however implicitly, that the present crisis was neither temporary nor "artificial," and that his policy would have to be geared toward some kind of restoration of the Union. Insofar as Lincoln was addressing Unionists (or potential Unionists) in the seceded states, he was assuming that war might still be avoided; insofar as he was addressing the border states, he was assuming that war was probably unavoidable and that he would need them.

Evincing hope that the crisis might yet be resolved, Lincoln's inaugural address attempted to strike a balance between firmness and conciliation. Lincoln reiterated ideas he had expressed for years and tried to show how they would guide his administration. He appealed to northerners and Unionists by insisting that the Union was perpetual and could not be disbanded by a disgruntled minority; that the Constitution and laws would be enforced; and that the authority of the federal government would be upheld. Conversely, he reached out to white southerners by emphasizing that the federal government was powerless to interfere with slavery in the states; that no effort at coercion or invasion would be attempted without provocation; and that he would exercise discretion and remain sensitive to local sentiment in upholding the national authority. While recognizing the sectional differences over slavery, Lincoln was at pains to convince white southerners that they still enjoyed all their traditional rights under the federal Constitution. He also insisted that slaveholders had no reason to fear a Republican administration, and that the interests of southerners in general and slaveholders in particular would be better served within the Union than outside it. Lincoln allowed for the people's right to revolution "whenever they shall grow weary of the existing government," but he reminded his listeners that constitutional remedies were available. And his famous peroration—invoking "our bonds of affection," "the mystic chords of memory," and "the better angels of our nature"—pulled at the heartstrings of all Americans.[2]

The inaugural address excluded explicit reference to "reconstruction" or "restoration," but it soon had special salience for reconstruction. Exactly four months later, in his July 4 message to the special session of Congress, Lincoln addressed the question of his policy toward the seceded states once the rebellion had been suppressed, thus indicating for the first time what a restored or reconstructed Union would look like. "Lest there be some uneasiness in the minds of candid men," he observed, "as to what is to be the course of the government, towards the Southern States, *after* the rebellion shall have been suppressed," he assured Congress and the nation that he would be guided by the Constitution and the law, and that he "probably will have no different understanding of the powers, and duties of the Federal government, relatively to the rights of the States, and the people, under the Constitution, than that expressed in the inaugural address." The failure to resolve the crisis peacefully did not initially cause Lincoln to envisage a fundamental redefining of the relations among the federal government, the states, and the people. Instead, reconstruction would involve restoring the traditional relations among them.[3]

The July 4 message to Congress also provided—along with his April 15 proclamation, issued immediately after the surrender of Fort

Sumter—Lincoln's overall conceptualization of the conflict and what would be required to end it. Lincoln confronted the Fort Sumter crisis immediately following his inauguration, and his refusal to surrender any federal posts effectively compelled Confederate forces to seize the fort before it could be resupplied. Having pledged not to attempt coercion without provocation, Lincoln was now presented with an overt defiance of federal authority that required forceful measures. The April 15 proclamation announced that, because the laws of the United States had been obstructed in the seceded states "by combinations too powerful to be suppressed by the ordinary course of judicial proceedings, or by the powers vested in the Marshals by law," Lincoln was calling forth seventy-five thousand state militia troops "to suppress said combinations, and to cause the laws to be duly executed." Their primary duty would "probably" be to repossess all federal properties and places that had been seized, Lincoln insisted, taking the utmost care "to avoid any devastation, any destruction of, or interference with, property, or any disturbance of peaceful citizens." Lincoln beseeched loyal citizens to support the federal government and ordered those opposing its authority to disperse and "retire peaceably" within twenty days. (The proclamation also called Congress into special session on July 4.) Lincoln thus initially interpreted secession as "combinations" of individuals acting together to subvert federal authority, and he envisioned reconstruction as the suppression of these combinations and the reassertion of that authority. Moreover, the "property" with which Lincoln pledged not to interfere was generally understood to include slavery.[4]

Lincoln's conceptualization of secession and the Confederacy held other important implications for reconstruction. By defining secession as rebellion and maintaining that the Confederacy had no legitimacy, Lincoln precluded the possibility of formal negotiations or communications between the federal and Confederate governments. Lincoln believed he had no discretion in adopting this course, since secession constituted a violation of the law that he as president was constitutionally obligated to enforce. (Neither was the possibility of foreign recognition of the Confederacy far from his mind.) Moreover, if the Confederate national government had no official existence, then it could never formally capitulate. Confederate military authorities could surrender to their federal counterparts, but Confederate civilian authorities could not. This may not have seemed a problem in 1861, but as the Confederacy continued to persist, and as the nature of the war itself changed, it would increasingly become one. The federal government's ultimate goal was to annihilate the Confederate national government and even, to the degree necessary, the Confederate state governments. During the war, Lincoln and Congress would confront the practical problem of establishing civilian governments in Union-occupied, former Confederate territory. One of Lincoln's greatest fears as the end of hostilities approached would be the possibility of conditions in the South degenerating into lawlessness once the Confederate government ceased to exist. By 1865, the closer the Union came to military victory, the more acute became the problem of determining exactly how Confederate civilian authorities, lacking an official existence, would capitulate.

Indeed, the status of state governments within the Confederacy proved to be among the most contentious of issues that Lincoln and northerners confronted. This question involved whether secession had been carried out by states or by "combinations" of individual persons. If states had seceded (in fact if not in theory), then the relations between them and the federal government had, in some fundamental way, been compromised, raising the question of how those relations were to be restored. Adhering to what Herman Belz has characterized as "territorialization," Radical Republicans especially argued that the Confederate states had reverted to "territorial" status (or were "conquered provinces," or had committed "state suicide") and thus could be administered directly by the federal government, and Congress in particular, before readmittance to the Union. What Belz has called "state indestructibility," by contrast, saw secession as the work of individuals acting through the framework of state governments, with the states essentially remaining unchanged. Reconstruction thus centered on dealing with these individuals and restoring relations between the seceded states and the federal government.

These views had important implications. Territorialization downplayed the distinction between loyal and disloyal citizens within each state, since the entire state, as the embodiment of the will of its people, had abrogated its normal relations with the Union. State indestructibility, by contrast, emphasized the distinction between a state's loyal and disloyal elements, and it saw the task of reconstruction as enabling the loyal element to regain control of the state government (or to create a new state government) in order to restore the state to the Union. Denying that states could ever leave the Union, Lincoln largely adhered to state indestructibility, despite the many practical difficulties this course engendered. Although he would eventually come to see the Confederacy as enjoying broad popular support, his sole deviation from state indestructibility involved the creation of the state of West Virginia in 1863.[5]

The theory of state indestructibility envisioned the eventual control of southern state governments by a vibrant Unionist element. Lincoln insisted in his July 4 message that Unionism was widespread in the South, especially in the upper South states of Virginia, North Carolina, Tennessee, and Arkansas, where "Union sentiment was nearly repressed, and silenced." All four states seceded only after Lincoln's April 15 proclamation, which they deemed coercive. Lincoln found the Virginia situation particularly troubling. There, a state convention that originally included a Unionist majority had met in mid-February and debated secession for weeks, with considerable opposition being expressed from the state's western counties. The beginning of hostilities radically shifted public sentiment, however, and the convention voted to secede on April 17, subject to a popular referendum on May 23. But for Lincoln, Virginia's leading men immediately began acting as though secession were already a fait accompli, seizing federal installations, allying the state with the Confederacy, and mobilizing for war. The outcome, he believed, was predictable, "for the result of an election, held in military camps, where the bayonets are all on one side of the question voted upon, can scarcely be considered as demonstrating popular sentiment." The state, in effect, had been railroaded out of the Union, leaving its loyalist population pleading for federal protection. Lincoln did not consider the situation much different in the lower South, save perhaps for South Carolina. "It may well be questioned whether there is, to-day, a majority of the legally qualified voters of any State, except perhaps South Carolina, in favor of disunion," he insisted in July. "There is much reason to believe that the Union men are the majority in many, if not in every other one, of the so-called seceded States."[6]

Whether Unionists were a majority in Virginia or in any other southern state, Virginia provided Lincoln with an opportunity to put his vision of reconstruction into practice, resulting in creation of that state's "Restored" government. Almost immediately following the state convention's vote to secede on April 17, Unionists in western Virginia, a number of whom were slaveholders who saw secession as a threat to slavery, undertook to call, with Lincoln's approval, their own convention in Wheeling. When the convention met in June, many delegates hoped to create a new state of their own, having long resented eastern dominance, but the majority recognized, as did Lincoln, the constitutional prohibition against altering a state's boundaries without its approval. The convention, which was dominated by the state's western counties but included Fairfax and Alexandria counties in the east, and which represented a quarter of the state's white population, created the "Restored Government of Virginia" and elected Francis Harrison Pierpont, a former Whig, as governor. Pierpont received Lincoln's support, and he called the state legislature into special session to elect US Senators. Lincoln approved of the new government in his July 4 message to Congress, and the two senators were seated (as were three previously elected Unionists by the House of Representatives), but not before conservative, border-state Democrats questioned the legitimacy of the Pierpont government on the grounds that only a majority of voters could represent a state. Perhaps the greatest legacy of the Pierpont government would be its role, as the official government of Virginia, in creating West Virginia. The Pierpont government could hardly be considered representative, but the Republican majority in Congress overwhelmingly approved it. In doing so, it endorsed Lincoln's vision of reconstruction as a speedy restoration of "so-called seceded" states to the Union by civilian governments under loyalist control.[7]

II

For Lincoln, restoration of the seceded states remained inseparable from conducting the war and maintaining public support for it. Even before the Union defeat at Bull Run in July, Lincoln had begun to conceptualize a broader military strategy that included taking advantage of the North's superior resources by attacking the Confederacy simultaneously on multiple fronts. Lincoln had not yet come to see the conflict as a war of attrition or as one against southern society at large, but, as James M. McPherson has argued, he began to grasp the larger dimensions of the war before his own generals had. In many respects, the story of Lincoln as commander-in-chief involves his search for generals who understood the war as he did and who could put that understanding into practice.[8]

In maintaining public support for the war, Lincoln balanced two overarching concerns. First, he had to hold together a war coalition that ranged from conservative Democrats who supported a war for the Union but opposed a war against slavery to abolitionists and Radical Republicans who implored Lincoln to wage war against slavery and criticized him for not doing so. Lincoln's initial course on slavery resulted from his belief that the federal government was powerless to act against slavery in the states, but it also owed to his second main consideration—keeping the border states of Delaware, Maryland, Kentucky, and Missouri in the Union. Although all four states had refused to secede, they were deeply divided and hosted significant slave populations and slaveholders who wielded considerable political influence. Lincoln believed that he could not afford to risk alienating the loyal slave states, especially Kentucky, by waging war on slavery. He maintained in his July 4 message that the border-state policy of "armed neutrality" provided greater assistance to the Confederacy than to the Union and amounted to "treason in effect," but for now he had to respect it. While Lincoln's original course on slavery in the Confederacy was dictated by solicitude for War Democrats and the border states, his move toward emancipation would be motivated by other considerations.[9]

The process by which Lincoln came to issue the Emancipation Proclamation has figured prominently in the historical scholarship on the Civil War, and it proved equally integral to his rethinking of reconstruction. Despite a congressional joint resolution of July 1861 affirming that the war was to preserve the Union and uphold the Constitution and not to interfere with slavery, the question of slavery soon became unavoidable. Almost from the beginning, slaves in tidewater Virginia took flight and sought refuge behind Union lines at Fortress Monroe, at the mouth of the James River. Although many contemporaries, North and South, expected Union soldiers to return the fugitive slaves of loyal owners, distinguishing between the slaves of loyal and disloyal slaveholders proved almost impossible. Moreover, because Confederate authorities had impressed many of these slaves as military laborers, Union general Benjamin F. Butler seized them as "contraband of war"—or "contrabands," as they came to be known. Congress addressed the conundrum of not interfering with slavery in the states even as slave property was being used for the rebellion by passing in early August 1861 the first confiscation act. This measure declared all property used in support of the rebellion the "subject of prize and capture," specifically including slaves used for military purposes. The act refrained from explicitly declaring these slaves free, but it nullified their masters' claim to them. However limited, this act rendered the federal policy of noninterference with slavery in the states untenable.[10]

Lincoln approved of Butler's "contraband" policy and signed the first confiscation act. However, he faced an imbroglio concerning slavery and the border states during the late summer and fall of 1861 over the actions of General John C. Frémont, commander of Union forces in Missouri. "The Pathfinder" to the West and the first Republican presidential candidate in 1856, Frémont boasted of antislavery credentials that made him a hero to the Radical Republicans. Facing an extremely volatile situation in that bitterly divided state, Frémont issued an order in late August declaring martial law statewide, which provided for the shooting of civilians convicted of bearing arms against the Union, and which declared free the slaves of disloyal slaveholders. After Frémont refused to comply with Lincoln's private request to modify his order so that it accorded with the recent confiscation act, Lincoln ordered him to do so. The Radicals were furious, but Lincoln justified his course by arguing that Frémont's order regarding slaves involved a *"purely political"* question, and that for generals to determine political policy was tantamount to "dictatorship." "It assumes that the general may do *anything* he pleases," he wrote, "confiscate the lands and free the slaves of *loyal* people, as well as disloyal ones."

Not only was it wrong in principle for generals to free slaves without authority of law, Lincoln reasoned, but it was also bad policy. Lincoln admitted that Frémont's order was popular in some quarters, "and would have been more so if it had been a general declaration of emancipation." However, in places such as Kentucky, where public sentiment overwhelmingly opposed the order, its effects would be far different. "I think to lose Kentucky is nearly the same as to lose the whole game," Lincoln famously observed. "Kentucky gone, we can not hold Missouri, nor, as I think Maryland." Not for the last time, Lincoln countermanded the order of a general who exceeded his authority concerning slavery. But the next time he did so, he expressed as much concern for his antislavery supporters as for his conservative ones, and far less concern with distinguishing between loyal and disloyal slaveholders.[11]

Lincoln's thinking on slavery, the war, and the border states assumes special relevance to reconstruction when viewed in conjunction with two other major initiatives to which he had been devoting considerable attention by late 1861, one for quite some time and the other only more recently. The former involved colonization and the latter compensated emancipation—a plan whereby the loyal slave states would abolish slavery of their own accord, with the federal government compensating loyal slaveholders for their lost property. These two interrelated initiatives, which helped move Lincoln toward emancipation, also contributed to the evolution of his approach to reconstruction.

Colonization has proven especially vexing to Lincoln scholars. Revisionists attempting to debunk Lincoln as the "Great Emancipator" have attached great significance to it, whereas Lincoln's defenders have downplayed it or have argued that it provided cover for Lincoln's antislavery principles. Yet Lincoln's commitment to colonization was indisputable and of long standing, and it reflected a viewpoint held by many Americans in the decades before the Civil War. While the colonizationists' motives were a mixture of racism, benevolence, and political opportunism, Lincoln's support for colonization owed to a sincere belief that white racism was immutable and would prevent black people from ever enjoying any measure of racial equality in America. Largely rejecting notions of innate racial inferiority and instead ascribing black people's inferior status to white animosity and slavery, Lincoln believed that black people could achieve a meaningful freedom only beyond the United States.[12]

Colonization might at first glance seem to have little relevance to Lincoln and reconstruction, and it has received limited attention in the literature on that topic. Yet even though Lincoln conceived of reconstruction by late 1861 and early 1862 as restoring the seceded states, colonization can still be seen as part of his larger vision of what a United States without slavery would look like. Lincoln always denied being an abolitionist and insisted that the federal government was powerless to attack slavery in the states. Yet equally central to his political philosophy was his belief that slavery be put on the road to ultimate extinction, and he envisioned this as a gradual process undertaken by the states with the federal government's assistance. One of the challenges Lincoln and other gradualists always faced from their conservative critics was the question of what would become of the former slaves after slavery had been abolished. Most nineteenth-century white Americans denied the possibility of a multiracial society and believed that the abolition of slavery must ultimately result either in a Darwinian race war or in racial "amalgamation." The only alternative was removal of the free black population. Lincoln always advocated voluntary rather than compulsory colonization, and he did not believe race war or amalgamation would inevitably result from emancipation. (Instead, black people would continue to occupy a subordinate status, and he did not foresee a solution to the problem that black people overwhelmingly opposed colonization.) Lincoln did not subscribe to the overt racism ubiquitous in his time, but during the first two years of his presidency, he envisioned a United States without slavery as one without black people.

As much as Lincoln insisted that the war was not about slavery, the implications of the 1861 confiscation act, along with the increasing number of fugitive slaves who could not be returned to slavery, made more immediate the problem of federal policy regarding former slaves. In his annual message to Congress in December 1861, Lincoln recommended "that steps be taken for colonizing" both those slaves already freed under the confiscation act and any other slaves whom the border states might liberate in the future. He also suggested including the nation's free black population in the proposal, though on a voluntary basis. Although Congress did not enact a colonization plan at this point, there was nonetheless considerable support among congressional Republicans for one, and Lincoln continued to push for colonization throughout 1862 and, though unofficially and more quietly, even after he issued the Emancipation Proclamation. Lincoln eventually dropped colonization as a key element of his vision for a restored Union and a reconstructed America, but for now it remained integral to that vision.[13]

Equally important to that vision was gradual, compensated emancipation for the border states, which Lincoln regarded as part of his larger, strategic plan for winning the war. As Lincoln saw the matter, an essential component of the Confederacy's own strategic thinking involved inducing the border states to secede and join the Confederacy. Or, the Confederacy might eventually compel the Union to negotiate and recognize Confederate independence, at which point the border states would likely join the newly independent Confederate States of America rather than remain in a failed United States. In either case, for Lincoln, the leaders of the rebellion pinned their hopes on winning over the border states. Thus, a plan that initiated the process of emancipation, however limited, would end any hope of the border states joining the Confederacy, dealing the rebellion a crushing blow.

Lincoln had suggested a compensated emancipation plan for Delaware as early as fall 1861. Although it gained little support, its failure prompted him to devise an even bolder initiative including all the border states. In his message to Congress of March 1862, he recommended passage of a joint resolution pledging federal financial assistance to states that adopted the "gradual abolishment of slavery." (Neither Lincoln's Delaware plan nor this proposal mentioned colonization.) Lincoln further argued, in this document and elsewhere, that compensated emancipation for the border states would cost far less than the war itself. Lincoln pledged that the plan would establish no federal claim to interfere with slavery in the states, but he also added a thinly veiled threat. Fully aware that the problem of fugitive slaves also affected the border states, and under intensifying pressure from radicals and abolitionists to attack slavery, he noted that should the rebellion continue, "it is impossible to foresee all the incidents, which may attend and all the ruin which may follow it. Such as may seem indispensable, or may obviously promise great efficiency towards ending the struggle, must and will come."[14]

Lincoln enlisted the aid of influential Republicans, radical and moderate, in garnering support for compensated, border-state emancipation. A few days after his congressional message, he met with a delegation of border-state congressmen to push his proposal. The congressmen, however, expressed skepticism over the plan's feasibility and constitutionality. Moreover, Congress in April 1862 passed Lincoln's joint resolution, but with the border-state members—who voted overwhelmingly against the resolution—showing no interest, Congress took no action, and the initiative stalled. Nonetheless, Congress that same month voted to abolish slavery in the District of Columbia while also authorizing funds to compensate owners and to colonize the former slaves. (No liberated slave accepted this colonization offer.) Believing that Congress always possessed the authority to abolish slavery in the district, Lincoln endorsed the measure, though he regretted that emancipation had been immediate rather than gradual. Lincoln's first effort in late 1861 and early 1862 to promote gradual, compensated emancipation in the border states along with colonization as a means to restoring the Union had failed. But Lincoln had been compelled to think seriously and concretely about a kind of reconstruction beyond simply restoring the antebellum status quo. Despite his efforts to reconcile a war for union with slavery, Lincoln was broaching the possibility that reconstruction might entail the transformation of slave society.[15]

III

Spring and summer 1862 witnessed one of the most dramatic developments of the entire war—Lincoln's deciding to issue a general proclamation declaring free the slaves in the seceded states. Military emancipation, despite its limitations, proved so central to reconstruction that one cannot be understood without reference to the other. Just as the Emancipation Proclamation transformed the war, Lincoln's military emancipation policy also compelled him to reconsider his approach to reconstruction. In this process, three factors were of particular significance: Lincoln's growing frustration over the inaction of southern Unionists and his larger reevaluation of southern Unionism; the outweighing of the border states and War Democrats by antislavery radicals, mainstream Republicans, and even slaves within the Union war coalition; and the blurring of the distinction between loyal and disloyal slaveholders in the Confederacy.

Lincoln's views on slavery and emancipation evolved during this period in tandem with those on Union military strategy. By early 1862, Lincoln and many northerners began expressing frustration with the Union military leadership's lack of vigor in prosecuting the war, especially in the cases of Generals George B. McClellan in the east and Don Carlos Buell in the west. Buell resisted Lincoln's entreaties to launch a campaign into eastern Tennessee to liberate the large Unionist population suffering at the hands of Confederates. McClellan's failures are the stuff of legend. His peninsular campaign, designed to capture Richmond, during the spring and summer; his overall lack of initiative; and his insistence on pursuing a limited war, to be conducted by professionals with minimal consequences for the South's white civilian population, helped convince Lincoln of the need for more vigorous war measures. Lincoln eventually concluded that his own conciliatory approach had to be replaced by a "hard war policy," though one tempered by magnanimity.[16]

Lincoln may have been frustrated with his generals, but the news in winter and spring 1862 was not all bad. General Ulysses S. Grant secured Union control of central Tennessee in February and northern Mississippi in April (at Shiloh), paving the way for the federal capture of Memphis in early June. Union forces moving up the Mississippi

River from the Gulf of Mexico managed to seize New Orleans by early May. Lincoln appointed Tennessee Unionist Andrew Johnson as military governor of that state, and he eventually appointed military governors for Louisiana, North Carolina, Arkansas, and other Confederate states where the federal military had established a foothold.

Lincoln's appointment of military governors for states, an unprecedented action in American history, was designed neither as part of a long-term military occupation nor to bring about radical change. Instead, it was to provide protection to Unionists, including slaveholders, so that they could organize and gain control of the state. The policy was also designed to undercut congressional efforts in early 1862 to enact territorialization legislation for the rebel states that would have opened the way for federal interference with slavery. Military rule under executive authority would serve as a temporary expedient toward the larger goal of restoring seceded states to the Union, but without prompting fundamental changes in their laws or institutions. Federal control would allow for the reassertion of Unionist sentiment that, in Lincoln's mind, secessionists had suppressed a year earlier. "If we could, somehow, get a vote of the people of Tennessee and have it result properly," Lincoln observed to Johnson, "it would be worth more than a battle gained."[17]

Yet the latent southern Unionism in which Lincoln had invested so much hope failed to materialize. Union military gains in North Carolina and Arkansas were too limited to engender the anticipated Unionist uprising. Johnson made some progress in central Tennessee and, to a lesser extent, in Memphis and western Tennessee, but Unionism was hamstrung by the inability of federal military forces to liberate eastern Tennessee. In a harbinger of future developments, moreover, Johnson's efforts to restore civilian government encountered interference from military authorities, forcing Johnson several times to bypass military commanders and appeal directly to Lincoln or Secretary of War Edwin M. Stanton. Worse still, difficulties in both Tennessee and North Carolina over enforcement of antebellum slave codes prompted congressional criticism of the principle of military governors and led, by early summer, to renewed attempts at territorialization.

Events in Louisiana caused Lincoln—not for the last time—
both headache and disappointment. Conditions in that state seemed
ripe for southern Unionism. Co-operationist sentiment had been
strong in parts of the state during the secession crisis, and Unionists had spoken openly at the secession convention. The situation
in New Orleans seemed especially promising. The Confederacy's
largest city, New Orleans hosted bloodthirsty secessionists but was
also home to transplanted northerners, immigrants, free persons
of color, and intellectuals who exhibited varying shades of Unionism. The mercantile community supported the Confederate cause
only moderately, and the allegiance of the state's influential sugar
planters, concerned with the protective tariff, was suspect. All these
factors caused Lincoln and many others to overestimate Unionist
sentiment in Louisiana.

The motives of many ostensible Unionists, moreover, might well
have been questioned. Complaining of the fugitive-slave problem,
which was widespread in Union-occupied Louisiana, as well as of
other disruptions, slaveholders appealed to Lincoln for relief. Though
avowing their loyalty, they displayed more concern with preserving
slavery than the Union. By late July, nearly three months after the
fall of New Orleans, Lincoln was expressing frustration with Louisiana affairs and signaling growing doubts about his policy toward
loyal slaveholders and southern Unionists in general. He had not yet
given up on southern Unionists, but his disenchantment with them
increased as he began to realize they were neither as numerous nor
as committed to the Union as he had assumed.

Lincoln's reassessment of southern loyalists was only part of his
larger reevaluation of the Union war coalition. To this point, Lincoln
had taken his Republican base (including Radical Republicans and
abolitionists) for granted, and he had bent over backwards trying
to conciliate southern slaveholders and retain the backing of the
border states and War Democrats. During the late spring and early
summer, however, he began to reverse those priorities, as evidenced
by his proclamation rescinding Union general David Hunter's order
of military emancipation, and by his renewed appeal to the border
states to adopt compensated emancipation.

Hunter commanded Union forces occupying Port Royal and parts of coastal South Carolina and Georgia, in the vicinity of Beaufort, which had been captured in November 1861. On May 9, without consulting Lincoln, Hunter saw fit to issue an order declaring "forever free" all slaves, not just those of disloyal owners, in South Carolina, Georgia, and Florida. As he had done earlier with John C. Frémont's emancipation order in Missouri, Lincoln countermanded Hunter's order. Yet in doing so, Lincoln announced that, should emancipation become necessary to the war effort, he alone as commander-in-chief had the authority to declare and implement such a policy. During the Frémont episode, Lincoln had denied that even he as president possessed this power, and his language in rescinding Hunter's shows that by this point he was moving decisively toward issuing an emancipation proclamation. Of equal significance, Lincoln called attention to his resolution, passed by Congress in April, proposing federal assistance to any state adopting gradual emancipation. In revoking Hunter's order, in fact, he devoted nearly as much attention to compensated emancipation as to the order itself. Lincoln was not quite ready to abandon compensated emancipation for the border states as a means to restoring the Union, but he clearly had more radical alternatives in mind.[18]

Hunter's order and its revocation caused Lincoln some political embarrassment. However, he managed to put the order to good use by renewing his appeal to the border states while also giving vent to the pressure he was under concerning slavery. On July 12, just as Congress was adjourning and only days before Lincoln informed the cabinet of his decision to issue a proclamation, he met with members of the border states' congressional delegations and urged them to persuade their constituents to adopt compensated emancipation. "The incidents of the war can not be avoided," Lincoln warned, and should the war continue much longer, "the institution [slavery] in your states will be extinguished by mere friction and abrasion." Slaves had already lost much of their value, Lincoln insisted, and would soon be worthless. Were the border states to adopt Lincoln's plan, which included colonization, slaveholders could salvage something and the Congressmen would be showing statesmanship.

Lincoln was not done. "I am pressed with a difficulty not yet mentioned—one which threatens division among those who, united are none too strong." An example of this "difficulty" was Hunter's recent proclamation, which Lincoln was forced to disavow. "Yet in repudiating it," he acknowledged, "I gave dissatisfaction, if not offence, to many whose support the country can not afford to lose." Lincoln was warning that the solicitude he had shown for the war coalition's conservative wing had alienated its antislavery element and even mainstream Republicans, who were coming to support emancipation out of military necessity if nothing else. This was the backbone of the Republican Party, whose support was essential to the war effort. "And this is not the end of it," Lincoln continued. "The pressure, in this direction, is still upon me, and is increasing." Although Lincoln had sympathized with Hunter's order, he was forced to revoke it, but the political cost had been high. No matter how important southern Unionists, loyal slaveholders, and the border states were to Lincoln's hopes for restoring the Union, Hunter's order represented the sentiments of those whose support Lincoln could not afford to lose.[19]

The third element of Lincoln's move toward emancipation that also reflected his rethinking of reconstruction—in addition to his disenchantment with southern Unionism and his reprioritizing of the war coalition—involved the increasingly untenable distinction between the Confederacy's loyal and disloyal slaveholders. From the outset, Lincoln defined secession as the work of "combinations" of individuals who had usurped the state governments, and he envisioned reconstruction as the process by which the loyal element within the seceded states, including slaveholders, might reassert control of those state governments and return the states to their proper relations to the Union. To this point, Lincoln had maintained the distinction between loyal and disloyal southerners, as had Congress. But as northern pressure continued for a war against slavery, as Lincoln and others saw the weakness of southern Unionism, and as the border states proved unresponsive to compensated emancipation, the previously important distinction between loyal and disloyal slaveholders in the seceded states seemed less relevant.

On July 17, for instance, Congress greatly expanded the scope of federal military emancipation by passing the second confiscation act, partly in response to the thousands of fugitive slaves in the Confederacy seeking shelter behind Union lines. This measure declared "forever free" the slaves of disloyal masters, ostensibly recognizing the distinction between loyal and disloyal owners. However, it also forbade military personnel from deciding on the validity of any slaveholder's claim to a fugitive, or from returning any fugitive slave to any claimant. The law thus effectively freed any fugitive slave, whether of a loyal or disloyal owner, who sought refuge behind Union lines, marking a major shift in Union policy. Although Lincoln opposed certain provisions of the act, he approved it, but, in a step unusual for its day, he also formally outlined his objections. These included Congress's asserting authority to free slaves in the states. As he had noted in revoking Hunter's emancipation order, and elsewhere, only the president, acting under the war power, possessed such authority. Lincoln also observed that the act made no provision for determining whether a fugitive slave belonged to a disloyal owner and thus would be immediately freed. Yet after calling attention to this apparently important omission, Lincoln brushed it aside, adding that the missing provision "could be easily supplied." Although Lincoln undertook to express his objections to this act, its effective blurring of the distinction between the Confederacy's loyal and disloyal slaveholders was not especially troubling.[20]

Several days later, Lincoln informed the cabinet of his decision to issue an emancipation proclamation for the seceded states, but he was persuaded to delay it until Union forces gained a victory. Meanwhile, he further prepared the public for emancipation. In mid-August, he met with a delegation of black leaders at the White House to promote colonization, thereby either reflecting his genuine commitment to colonization or shrewdly covering his political flank. He also issued his famous letter to Horace Greeley, avowing that his goal was to preserve the Union and that he would do so by freeing none, all, or some of the slaves. Although Lincoln still distinguished between loyal and disloyal slaveholders in the seceded states, a distinction that had been central to his vision of reconstruction, he had laid the groundwork for a proclamation that ultimately eliminated that distinction. In balancing between those who would reconstruct the Union by preserving slavery and those who would do so by destroying it, Lincoln had generally sided with the former, but he was now about to join the ranks of the latter. As Robert E. Lee took his army into Maryland in early September, Lincoln hoped for the military victory that—even if it did not end the war—would allow him to change the meaning of the war, and of reconstruction.[21]

IV

The battle of Antietam on September 17 gave Lincoln the needed "victory." In what came to be known as the preliminary emancipation proclamation, Lincoln on September 22 announced his intention to proclaim "forever free" all slaves in areas in rebellion against the United States as of January 1, 1863. He thus extended to the seceded states one final opportunity to resume their place in the Union with slavery intact, while making clear that, should they not avail themselves of this opportunity, wholesale military emancipation, if not necessarily the outright abolition of slavery, would become the means for restoring the Union. Lincoln's words during this period indicate how closely reconstruction had become linked to emancipation, with the latter functioning both as inducement and threat. States (or parts thereof) that returned to the Union before the January 1 deadline would escape having their slaves freed, while those that did not return would not.

Lincoln began the proclamation by sounding familiar themes. He declared that "hereafter, as heretofore, the war will be prosecuted for the object of practically restoring the constitutional relation between the United States, and each of the states, and the people thereof." He would again recommend congressional approval of compensated emancipation for loyal slaveholding states, adding that the promotion of voluntary colonization would also be continued. Lincoln then announced that on January 1, 1863, "all persons held as slaves" within any state or part thereof in rebellion against the United States "shall be then, thenceforward, and forever free." To implement this policy, Lincoln on that date would formally designate, by proclamation, those states or parts thereof in rebellion against the United States. Any state represented in Congress at that time—by members chosen at elections in which a majority of its qualified voters participated—would be deemed not in rebellion and excluded from the proclamation. Lincoln then called attention to the congressional article of war passed in March 1862, prohibiting federal military personnel from returning fugitive slaves, and to the 1862 confiscation act further strengthening that policy, and he ordered military personnel to obey and enforce these laws. In the final section, Lincoln indicated he would support compensation for loyal slaveholders, including those in seceded states that rejoined the Union.[22]

Just as the proclamation marked a cataclysmic change in the meaning of the war, it also reflected an essential shift in Lincoln's approach to reconstruction. Whereas Lincoln had originally defined secession as the work of "combinations" of individuals, he would now declare entire geographical areas to be in rebellion, irrespective of individual loyalties. Lincoln still adhered to state indestructibility, and the distinction between loyal and disloyal citizens remained integral to state restoration. Nonetheless, not only were there fewer Unionists in the Confederate states than Lincoln had thought, but the rebellion had also assumed a collective identity that transcended the actions of individuals working together. Because the Confederacy, in essence, enjoyed broad popular support, restoring seceded states to the Union would involve more than shepherding a (non-existent) Unionist majority into power. Similarly, the distinction between loyal and disloyal slaveholders would be obliterated. Even loyal slaveholders would lose their slaves. Lincoln pledged to support compensation for loyal slaveholders, but as far as their status as slaveholders per se was concerned, the distinction between loyal and disloyal was irrelevant, as was the role of loyal slaveholders in reconstruction. Indeed, once the Emancipation Proclamation had been issued in final form, the very idea of a loyal slaveholder in the Confederacy ceased to exist.

One element of the preliminary proclamation especially relevant to reconstruction involved the method by which Lincoln would designate former Confederate areas not in rebellion on January 1.

Although differences between Lincoln (and other supporters of state indestructibility) and congressional advocates of territorialization had become evident, a consensus emerged by mid-summer 1862 around the view that electing members to Congress constituted the most practical method of restoring seceded states to the Union. This policy also gained ground when Congress adjourned in July without enacting reconstruction legislation, largely owing to Democratic and conservative-Republican opposition to territorialization. Throughout the summer Lincoln had pushed his military governors and other federal authorities in occupied areas to work with Unionists in organizing congressional elections, and he redoubled those efforts during the fall, hoping the threat of military emancipation might hasten state restoration. Elections would eventually take place in parts of North Carolina (after January 1), Tennessee and Virginia, but once again Louisiana assumed center stage. In December, almost seventy-eight hundred voters in that state's first and second congressional districts, near New Orleans, participated in elections won by Unionists Benjamin Flanders and Michael Hahn. This total amounted to roughly half the ballots cast in those districts in the last antebellum congressional election, lending the results some legitimacy and partly assuaging Lincoln's concern that the elections reflect the sentiments of the state's "respectable citizens" and not appear a sham perpetrated by "our military and quasi-military, authorities." Although Lincoln had revised his thinking on southern Unionism, and although reconstruction and emancipation were now linked, the preliminary proclamation was designed to promote reconstruction by at least allowing the seceded states the opportunity to avoid wholesale emancipation.[23]

This provision raised a host of issues that would remain central to reconstruction. Perhaps the most obvious was whether the abolition of slavery would be a condition for state readmission after January 1, but this led to the question of what other conditions relevant to emancipation might be imposed on the former Confederate states. If holding congressional elections was the benchmark for loyalty, moreover, would Congress or the president oversee the elections, and thus was the process of reconstruction an executive or legislative function? While participation in congressional elections would be limited to those who had taken a loyalty oath, to what degree could elections function as a barometer of a state's loyalty? Was it realistic to require a majority of a state's qualified voters to participate in the elections, especially within so short a time frame and in light of Lincoln's own recognition that the Confederacy enjoyed popular support? Would members-elect from formerly seceded states automatically be seated in Congress, and thus would Congress simply rubber-stamp presidential initiative? By including in a presidential proclamation a provision requiring congressional action, Lincoln had created a difficult problem involving separation of powers: Congress's role in reconstruction might be either superfluous or obstructionist. Indicative of these difficulties, the final proclamation would exempt Tennessee and Union-occupied parts of Louisiana and Virginia (including the soon-to-be state of West Virginia) even though they had not met Lincoln's requirements, and Congress would debate the seating of their members-elect into 1863.

While the preliminary proclamation offered the seceded states one last chance to return to the Union with slavery, Lincoln in early December made his final appeal to them in his annual message to Congress, unquestionably one of the most bizarre documents of his entire presidency. Lincoln again proposed gradual, compensated emancipation and colonization, this time to the seceded states as well. The proposal served as an extended summary of Lincoln's approach to reconstruction to this point, while also peering decades into the future. Lincoln hoped to end the war and restore the seceded states by inducing southern loyalists to elect members to Congress by January 1. The proclamation, which the annual message did not mention, would thus be rendered moot, and the formerly seceded states might even participate in compensated emancipation along with the border states—where Lincoln believed slavery was doomed anyway. The whole thing was held together, as had been true of emancipationist schemes for decades, by colonization. However impossible the plan looks with the benefit of hindsight, or seemed to many contemporaries, Lincoln was not only trying to end the war but also offering an almost futuristic vision—projecting as far forward as 1930—of a re-United States.

Lincoln began by again promoting colonization. While admitting that black Americans and the foreign nations most likely to receive them had shown little interest in it, he nonetheless believed opinion among the former was "improving." He then devoted several paragraphs to exploring the meaning of nationhood, arguing that the United States possessed no natural boundaries that would sustain a separation into two independent nations, and concluding that "our strife pertains to ourselves—to the passing generations of men; and it can, without convulsion, be hushed forever with the passing of one generation." Perhaps overly sanguine on the prospects of resolving difficulties that had plagued the nation since its founding, Lincoln turned to the heart of his proposal: three constitutional amendments, along with a rationale for each. The first provided federal compensation to any loyal state that abolished slavery by 1900; the second guaranteed the freedom of all slaves liberated during the war and provided compensation to their owners who had remained loyal; and the third authorized congressional funding for voluntary colonization.

In defending the initiative, Lincoln acknowledged "great diversity, of sentiment, and of policy, in regard to slavery, and the African race amongst us," and that "we waste much strength in struggles among ourselves." Instead, "we should harmonize, and act together" by working toward "mutual concession." "This would be compromise," he noted, "but it would be compromise among the friends, and not with the enemies of the Union. These articles are intended to embody a plan of such mutual concessions." Were the plan to be adopted, "it is assumed that emancipation will follow, at least, in several of the States." Lincoln recognized that no seceded state was likely to lay down its arms by January 1, but he could not entirely discount the possibility of even one doing so, thereby keeping slavery for the time being and eventually benefitting from compensated emancipation, while at the same time furthering discord within the Confederacy. (Lincoln made no provision for seceded states that returned to the Union by January 1 but did not abolish slavery by 1900.)

In explicating the proposed amendments, Lincoln devoted most attention to the one on compensated emancipation, which was also the most visionary, not to say fantastical. He argued that by allowing emancipation to occur over thirty-seven years, "the advocates of per-petual slavery . . . will have passed away before its consummation. They will never see it." The slaves would also benefit, since gradual emancipation "saves them from the vagrant destitution which must largely attend immediate emancipation in localities where their num-bers are very great; and it gives the inspiring assurance that their posterity shall be free forever." The plan would leave states in control of abolishing slavery and compensating slaveholders, thus mitigating "the dissatisfaction of those who favor perpetual slavery, and espe-cially of those who are to receive compensation." Lincoln defended compensation on the grounds that slaves were property—an idea he had always reluctantly conceded—and that "in a sense the liberation of slaves is the destruction of property"; and, anticipating an idea he would make famous, he insisted that the entire nation was complicit in slavery and responsible for eradicating it. Lincoln then undertook an extended demographic analysis to argue that population growth through 1900—when he estimated the US population would reach more than one hundred million—would make compensated eman-cipation less expensive to future generations than was the cost of the war to the current generation of some thirty million. Indeed, he insisted, the nation's population might number more than two hun-dred million by 1930, "if we do not ourselves relinquish the chance, by the folly and evils of disunion, or by long and exhausting war springing from the only great element of national discord among us." Thus, "the proposed emancipation would shorten the war, perpetuate peace, insure this increase of population, and proportionately the wealth of the country." In sum, "a dollar will be much harder to pay for the war, than will be a dollar for emancipation on the proposed plan. And then the latter will cost no blood, no precious life. It will be a saving of both."

Having paid so much attention to compensated emancipation, Lincoln devoted one short paragraph to the article guaranteeing the freedom of slaves already emancipated—calling it "impracticable to return them to bondage"—and compensating their owners, if loyal. And in elaborating on the colonization amendment, Lincoln reaffirmed his support for the policy, yet he also insisted that the "objection urged against free colored persons remaining in the country" was "largely imaginary, if not sometimes malicious." He then devoted the entirety of what was ostensibly an argument supporting colonization to debunking two of the more incendiary claims made by emancipation's northern opponents—that free black labor would undercut white labor, and that liberated slaves would head north in droves. Lincoln's defenders might justifiably contend that this was a poor argument for colonization.

Lincoln concluded the annual message by addressing some of the implications of his proposal for the war and reconstruction. The plan was a recommendation and not a requirement the seceded states must accept in submitting to federal authority, yet neither the war nor the preliminary emancipation proclamation would be halted because of it. "Its timely *adoption*, I doubt not, would bring restoration and thereby stay both." The current proposal did not negate the one Lincoln had recommended in March, which Congress had approved by resolution, and it was a supplement to, not an exclusive substitute for, all other plans for restoring the national authority. Anticipating the issue that would arise over the future amendment abolishing slavery, Lincoln maintained that the number of states necessary for ratification of his proposal should include the seceded states, meaning some of them would have to ratify the amendments for them to be adopted. Finally, Lincoln in his peroration called on Congress and the nation to support his proposal, expressing some of the most memorable sentiments in the Lincoln lexicon: "The dogmas of the quiet past, are inadequate to the stormy present"; "As our case is new, so must we think anew, and act anew"; "Fellow-citizens, *we* cannot escape history"; and, "In *giving* freedom to the *slave*, we *assure* freedom to the *free*—honorable alike in what we give, and what we preserve. We shall nobly save, or meanly lose, the last best, hope of earth."[24]

Lincoln envisioned his compensated emancipation proposal as a reasonable, integrated attempt to end the war, offering incentives to the seceded states to return to the Union and to the border states to abolish slavery. He probably did not expect the seceded states to accept the plan, but he also believed he had to give them every opportunity to return to the Union before issuing the final proclamation. He undoubtedly extended the overture in good faith and not as political cover for a preconceived determination to implement emancipation. To Lincoln, the whole thing made sense. And yet, he also seemed to be missing the point. Slavery was never just a system of property rights, never just about economics and money. Instead, slavery represented a way of life and conceptualization of the world, one he was asking the present generation of white southerners to abandon, for themselves and their descendants. Lincoln even admitted in the annual message that "the subject is presented exclusively in its economical aspect." This was an odd perspective for someone with such an ability to see the world as others did, who, unlike many of the abolitionists, insisted that slavery should be condemned but not the slaveholders, and who suggested that had northerners been raised and lived in the South they too would support slavery. Still, there is no denying the earnestness of the appeal. Lincoln may have been fully aware that slavery involved more than just money and property; and yet, by presenting the subject in its "economical aspect," he made the offer based on what he ultimately believed were the slaveholders' terms. He very likely expected the seceded states to reject his plan even as he held out hope that they might accept it.

So long as they could sustain armies in the field, the seceded states had no compelling reason to accept Lincoln's offer. What slim hopes it may have had were dashed on December 13 in the disastrous Union defeat at Fredericksburg, the latest in a string of setbacks Lincoln, Republicans, and the Union cause had recently suffered. Others included the Sioux uprising in Minnesota, criticism over again suspending habeas corpus, the fall midterm elections, and relieving McClellan from command—and to which would be added the mid-December cabinet crisis over Secretary of State William H. Seward's threatened resignation (which Lincoln successfully resolved). Meanwhile, Lincoln continued to pursue reconstruction. He encouraged southern Unionists to hold congressional elections and signed legislation creating West Virginia. In an act that would have important implications, he let stand a ruling by Attorney General Edward Bates in November affirming that free black people were American citizens, effectively nullifying the *Dred Scott* decision. Conversely, he also agreed to a plan to colonize several hundred black people on an island off the coast of Haiti. The only colonization initiative undertaken during Lincoln's presidency, it would fail miserably by early 1864. But on January 1, 1863, Lincoln changed American history by signing the Emancipation Proclamation.

While the proclamation remains among the most important documents in American history, the differences between the preliminary and final versions had important implications for reconstruction. The final proclamation excluded all of Tennessee and most of the Union-occupied parts of Louisiana and Virginia, even though these places had not fully met Lincoln's requirements in the preliminary proclamation. By contrast, the final proclamation applied to other Union-occupied areas, such as coastal North and South Carolina, where little or no progress had been made in meeting those requirements. The final proclamation included no provision for compensating loyal slaveholders within the Confederacy, as had the preliminary version, and it contained a short paragraph enjoining those slaves who gained their freedom to refrain from violence while also recommending that, "in all cases when allowed, they labor faithfully for reasonable wages." In however limited a sense, Lincoln was clearly indicating that reconstruction would entail, in addition to restoring the national authority over the seceded states, the broader transformation of the South's social and economic relations.[25]

Perhaps the most significant differences between the two proclamations were the elimination of colonization in the final version coupled with the announcement that black men would be enlisted into the federal armed forces. Lincoln thus broke the historic link between emancipation and colonization, and he opened the door to one of the strongest arguments—military service—that the proponents of racial equality would make after the war. In a larger sense, Lincoln greatly contributed to the historic transformation of black people in America from "persons of African descent," alienated from or outside of American society, to African Americans. Reconstruction henceforth would entail the restoration of the seceded states as well as the redefining of the place of black people within American society. As Eric Foner has observed, "the proclamation launched the historical process of Reconstruction. A new system of labor, politics, and race relations would have to replace the shattered institution of slavery."[26]

Some scholars argue that Lincoln's vision of reconstruction throughout the war is better described as restoration. His main goal, they contend, always involved restoring the national authority over the seceded states, with Unionists in control of the state governments and with no significant changes in the traditional relations between the states and the federal government or within southern society at large. This approach is said to contrast with more radical visions, which advocated fundamental transformations on these matters and called for the Union to be not restored but reconstructed. Lincoln's limited approach transcended even the Emancipation Proclamation, it is said, the limitations of which reflected his goal of suppressing rebellion and restoring states rather than undertaking wholesale reconstruction. Even in destroying slavery, Lincoln was trying to restore and not reconstruct.[27]

Although this argument has considerable merit, it mistakenly emphasizes the continuities in Lincoln's approach to reconstruction over the essential discontinuities. To be sure, from Fort Sumter to Appomattox, Lincoln remained transfixed on restoring federal authority over the seceded states. Thus, the means employed to achieve that end, including military emancipation, must be viewed within that context. Nonetheless, this viewpoint is difficult to reconcile with the Emancipation Proclamation and its implications. Slavery constituted the very foundation of southern antebellum society and, as Confederate vice president Alexander H. Stephens proclaimed, the cornerstone of the Confederacy. Its destruction therefore inaugurated a revolutionary transformation of the distinct social order to which it gave rise. Although the Emancipation Proclamation did not formally abolish slavery as an institution, it irrevocably linked slavery's ultimate demise to that of the Confederacy. Even as the proclamation transformed the meaning of the war, it also helped to alter Lincoln's restorationist mindset to one of genuine reconstruction.

FROM EMANCIPATION TO
RECONSTRUCTION
(January–December 1863)

Even as it redefined the Civil War, the Emancipation Proclamation presented Lincoln with two distinct but interrelated
difficulties concerning reconstruction. However transformative,
the proclamation raised the question of whether abolishing slavery
would become a condition for the Confederate states' readmission to
the Union. Many people at the time, including Lincoln, wondered
about the proclamation's fate once peace returned. Yet even allowing
for its validity, the proclamation freed slaves in the rebellious states
but did not abolish slavery as an institution. As unlikely as it may
seem, the possibility of seceded states returning to the Union after
January 1, 1863, while refusing to abolish slavery represented more
than a hypothetical problem. Some concrete policy would have to be
devised that precluded such an outcome. Determining the process
of restoring seceded states to the Union was hardly a new problem
in 1863, but the proclamation greatly complicated it.

The proclamation also created a dilemma for Lincoln. Military
success during 1863 helped to strengthen Union resolve, but it also
had the unanticipated consequence of sparking calls from northern
conservatives, War Democrats especially, to open negotiations with
the Confederacy. Claiming that a weakened Confederate government might be amenable to peace talks, or even that individual
states might be lured back to the Union, Lincoln's northern critics

insisted that the primary obstacle to peace and reunion was not the Confederacy itself but rather the Emancipation Proclamation. This argument carried less weight during the first half of the year, when the war was going poorly for the North, than it did after Union victories at Gettysburg and Vicksburg in July and later in eastern Tennessee. In response, Lincoln initiated a public relations campaign in defense of emancipation in early 1863, and he redoubled those efforts in the late summer and fall, as Union success increased the pressure to negotiate. Having rejected negotiations from the first, and having finally issued the Emancipation Proclamation, Lincoln took pains to remind northerners that emancipation was not a mere bargaining chip.

This dilemma had a southern dimension. Having predicated his entire war policy on the legal fiction that the seceded states had never left the Union, Lincoln now faced the possibility of their accepting his pre–Emancipation Proclamation offer of submitting to federal authority with slavery intact. Alternatively, the seceded states might even agree to abide by the proclamation and yet refuse to abolish slavery in hopes of a future revival. Despite a wealth of scholarship on conflict within the Confederacy, an equally rich literature on Confederate nationalism has demonstrated that Confederate leaders were unlikely ever to have accepted a negotiated settlement short of independence. Nonetheless, Lincoln worried about a possible Confederate peace overture with slavery, which he knew would have wide appeal in the North. Although the proclamation did not abolish slavery, Lincoln now saw abolition as a condition of state readmission, even as it remained unclear how that goal would be achieved. Lincoln had rejected negotiations from the start, but the proclamation amounted to a demand for "unconditional surrender." He therefore had reason to fear a conditional surrender—and a restoration of the Union—based on preserving slavery.

Lincoln expended much effort throughout 1863 on these two difficulties. In addition to his public defense of emancipation, he further encouraged southern Unionists and former Confederates to return their states to the Union, but now without slavery. He would even accept gradual emancipation rather than insisting on immediate.

However, the disappointing results in trying to link state restoration to the abolition of slavery prompted Lincoln to issue in early December his Proclamation of Amnesty and Reconstruction, as part of his annual message. The "ten-percent plan" has come to be seen as Lincoln's blueprint for reconstruction. Whether it was his definitive word on the subject, it offered a solution to the two difficulties his emancipation policy caused for his approach to reconstruction: establishing the abolition of slavery as a condition for state restoration, and preempting any negotiated settlement that included the preservation of slavery.

I

Following December's Fredericksburg debacle, Union military fortunes hardly improved in early 1863. Dissension was rife among the officers of the Army of the Potomac. After January's infamous "Mud March," Union commander Ambrose E. Burnside attempted to have several subordinate generals removed, but Lincoln instead replaced Burnside with Joseph E. Hooker. His moniker "Fighting Joe" raised hopes for military success, and Lincoln appointed him despite his having recently declared that the country needed a dictator. Lincoln gave Hooker time to reorganize his command and rebuild morale, but Hooker soon evinced a disturbing hesitancy. Much like McClellan, moreover, and to Lincoln's consternation, he spoke more of taking Richmond than of smashing Lee's army. Meanwhile, General William S. Rosecrans, who had replaced Don Carlos Buell in the west the previous fall, made little progress in what Lincoln hoped would be a campaign to liberate eastern Tennessee's Unionists and restore the state. Ulysses S. Grant's Vicksburg campaign likewise seemed to be going nowhere after several failed initiatives. By mid-April, he had cut his supply lines, moved his army south of the city, and disappeared. Back east, when Hooker finally mobilized in early May, the result was another catastrophe inflicted by Robert E. Lee, this time at Chancellorsville. "What will the country say?" Lincoln lamented when he heard the news. By late June, Lee again threatened to invade the North, and Lincoln replaced Hooker with George Gordon Meade. Reconstruction seemed moot.

These setbacks notwithstanding, Congress intensely debated reconstruction. On convening in December 1862, it considered several matters that followed from earlier developments. The most important involved seating members-elect from areas of the seceded states where congressional elections had been held, on which basis those areas had been excluded from the Emancipation Proclamation. The key southern claimants were Michael Hahn and Benjamin Flanders, from Louisiana's first and second districts. Although Democrats and some Radical Republicans challenged the validity of the elections, arguing they had taken place under executive and even military authority, the Louisiana claimants were seated. Those from Virginia, Tennessee, and North Carolina, whose elections came nowhere near eliciting the majority of voters the preliminary emancipation proclamation had specified, were denied. Still, seating Flanders and Hahn was a major victory for Lincoln, one that could serve as a precedent for reconstruction in general and help launch a loyal Louisiana government.[1]

In seating Flanders and Hahn, Congress signaled its willingness to work with Lincoln on reconstruction. Yet members also asserted their independence by considering legislation governing congressional elections and the creation of new governments for the seceded states. Congress ultimately adjourned without enacting this legislation, but the debates over it, as well as those over seating the southern claimants, revealed an emerging Republican consensus on reconstruction. Although the previous year's debates over territorialization and state indestructibility favored the latter, many Republicans were coming to agree that Congress could influence reconstruction through the constitutional guarantee of a republican form of government in the states. It therefore possessed the authority to establish procedures and set the conditions for readmitting the seceded states. Despite differences on many specifics, moreover, congressional Republicans also generally concurred that the conditions for readmittance include not only abolishing slavery but also creating new state governments with free-state constitutions, prohibiting former Confederates from office, and repudiating Confederate debt. Following Congress's March adjournment, northern debate reflected considerable support for abolishing slavery as an essential condition of reconstruction.[2]

The effort to couple state restoration with the abolition of slavery received reinforcement with the creation of West Virginia, however anomalous its situation. Adhering to the constitutional proscription against changing a state's boundaries without its permission, Virginia's Pierpont government in late 1861 commenced the process of severing the area that would become West Virginia, even though this was virtually the only part of Virginia the Pierpont government represented. By July 1862, the US Senate passed legislation creating the new state, and in December the House did the same, although the bill postponed admission until its constitution provided for the abolition of slavery. Lincoln signed the bill into law on the last day of 1862, and in early 1863 voters in the prospective state approved a constitution gradually abolishing slavery. West Virginia formally became a state in June 1863, and it abolished slavery entirely in early 1865.

Because the creation of West Virginia was unique—the only instance in US history of secession from an existing state to create a new one—its relevance to reconstruction can be overlooked. Yet the Virginia–West Virginia situation had important implications for Lincoln's approach to reconstruction. In one sense, West Virginia seemed to confirm Lincoln's original vision of reconstruction as a process whereby Unionists in a particular geographical region of the Confederacy, if not an entire state, would seize the initiative in restoring their state to the Union—and, after January 1863, providing for the abolition of slavery. Yet it also contradicted that vision. Along with violating (quite literally) the principle of state indestructibility, severing the loyal part of a seceded state also undermined the prospects of restoring the original state under loyalist auspices. Doing so might even make that task more difficult, since it removed a significant portion of the loyalist element from the original state and made its remainder more thoroughly Confederate. Pretending that the Pierpont government—which for many was something of a joke—represented all white Virginians before the creation of West Virginia was questionable enough, but *whom* would that government now represent? And yet, West Virginia also shared much with other Unionist enclaves within the Confederacy, such as eastern Tennessee and western North Carolina. Creating West Virginia established a precedent that could conceivably be followed in other instances, and it opened the door to more radical versions of territorialization, including the obliteration of the seceded states' boundaries and their reconfiguration as entirely new states. [3]

Lincoln addressed some of these issues in his opinion on admitting West Virginia, written, after much deliberation and consultation, the day he signed the statehood bill into law. Lincoln reduced the matter to questions of constitutionality and political expediency. He justified the first largely on the legitimacy of the (loyal) Virginia legislature that consented to creating West Virginia. Admitting that a majority of the qualified voters had not participated in its election, he insisted that it was the qualified voters "*who choose to vote*, that constitute the political power of the state." Those not voting did so either out of neglect or because they were engaged in rebellion, thus it would be absurd to equate their sentiments with those who displayed their loyalty by voting. In addition to deliberate nonvoters were Unionists prevented from voting. "Doubtless among these non-voters were some Union men whose voices were smothered by the more numerous secessionists," Lincoln acknowledged, "but we know too little of their number to assign them any appreciable value." This was light-years from Lincoln's 1861 insistence that Unionists were a majority in the seceded states, save South Carolina, and that secession was the work of a political minority. It also contradicted the preliminary emancipation proclamation's principle of a *majority* of voters as a measure of Unionism. Though Lincoln now believed that the Confederacy enjoyed popular support, it remained unclear what consequences such support would have for placing Unionists in control in the seceded states. Just as Lincoln's advocacy of the Pierpont government presupposed an almost willful denial that West Virginia hosted the large majority of Virginia Unionists, it also ignored the implications that creating West Virginia would have for the viability of the Pierpont government. Indeed, while West Virginia moved toward statehood in early 1863, Congress refused to seat Virginia's claimants.

Lincoln was on firmer ground considering West Virginia statehood as a matter of expediency—whether admission, as he put it, would "under all circumstances tend the more strongly to the restoration of the national authority throughout the Union." He admitted that creating West Virginia would likely make Virginia's restoration more difficult by solidifying Confederate sentiment there. Still, this difficulty had to be weighed against the gain to the Unionist cause by adding West Virginia and the loss to it by rejecting statehood. "We can scarcely dispense with the aid of West-Virginia in this struggle; much less can we afford to have her against us, in congress and in the field." West Virginians had endured great hardship and demonstrated their fealty to the Union, and so the federal government, having held out the promise of statehood, could not "break faith with them." Admitting West Virginia, moreover, "turns that much slave soil to free" and would deal another blow to the rebellion. Lincoln allowed that dividing a state created a troubling precedent, yet he maintained that "a measure made expedient by a war," as with West Virginia, "is no precedent for times of peace." Finally, responding to criticism that the West Virginia situation constituted secession and was "tolerated only because it is our secession," he insisted that "there is still difference enough between secession against the constitution, and secession in favor of the constitution." West Virginia may have represented, as Herman Belz has observed, "a kind of reconstruction," but it served as a poor precedent for state restoration. Ultimately, neither Virginia's Pierpont government nor the new state of West Virginia solved the problem of Confederate armies in the field.[4]

Whatever constitutional questions it raised, West Virginia statehood stood as a success in restoring former Confederate territory to the Union with provisions for abolishing slavery. It certainly showed greater progress during the first half of 1863 than was true of either Tennessee or Louisiana, two other Confederate states where Lincoln hoped Unionists would translate military success into reconstruction.

Although Union general William S. Rosecrans drove Confederate forces from Murfreesboro in late 1862, solidifying Union control of central Tennessee, military governor Andrew Johnson believed it inexpedient to hold statewide elections and restore the state until eastern Tennessee had been secured and its large Unionist population could participate in electing a loyal government. Despite Tennessee's exclusion from the Emancipation Proclamation, Johnson supported Lincoln's emancipation policy; and although he believed that policy hurt Unionism in Tennessee, he was confident it would not seriously hamper restoration. By early summer, however, Johnson faced a political insurgency of conservative Unionists in western and central Tennessee, who pushed for elections for a state government and members of Congress under the antebellum constitution, to be held in August (presumably before eastern Tennessee could be liberated). Their goals were to replace Johnson—and his support for emancipation and proscriptive measures against rebels—and to take advantage of Tennessee's exemption from the proclamation to restore the state with slavery intact. Johnson fended off the initial phase of this attack, but he continued to be embroiled in political warfare with conservative Unionists, and Tennessee reconstruction stalled for the rest of the year owing to the federal military's failure to liberate eastern Tennessee.[5]

Louisiana reconstruction fared little better. The capture of New Orleans the previous April had spawned a fledgling Unionist movement under Generals Benjamin F. Butler, a Massachusetts political appointee and military department commander, and George F. Shepley, the military governor. Although Butler had induced several thousand residents to swear allegiance, his confrontational style did little to foster Unionism. In his defense, Butler could be credited with having organized congressional elections (that permitted the exclusion of New Orleans and its environs from the Emancipation Proclamation) and having brought effective government to the city. Nonetheless, by late 1862 he had so alienated various constituencies in New Orleans that Lincoln replaced him with Nathaniel P. Banks, another Massachusetts political general who had served as the first Republican Speaker of the US House of Representatives. Banks envisioned himself as a mediator among the differing interests in Union-held Louisiana, and Lincoln probably hoped his conciliatory style would facilitate the state's restoration. Bitter political conflict among Unionists, however, would stall any substantive progress.

By early 1863, two groups of Unionists had emerged to vie for control over reconstruction in Louisiana. First, the Free State organization was a diverse coalition of local radicals, immigrants, and transplanted northerners, some of whom had resided in the state for years. Internally divided between radicals and moderates, the organization agreed on emancipation but not on other matters involving race. Its members wanted to hold a state convention that, before electing a government, would write a new constitution abolishing slavery, and they proposed undertaking a registry of loyal citizens for the purpose of electing delegates to the convention. The election would not require a majority of voters in each parish (county) but instead would involve a small loyalist core, and representation at the convention would be determined not by total population, which would include slaves, but by the white population only. This provision would bolster the Unionist and antislavery element in New Orleans while undermining the disproportionate influence slaveholding planters had enjoyed under Louisiana's antebellum constitutions. The other group, the Conservative Unionists, included sugar planters and New Orleans businessmen who had taken the loyalty oath and hoped to preserve both the antebellum constitution and slavery. Seizing on the exclusion of Union-occupied Louisiana from the Emancipation Proclamation, and arguing that slavery was still legal, they proposed holding elections under the existing constitution for members to the next Congress (to convene in December 1863). They ultimately hoped to form a new state government that would restore Louisiana to the Union with slavery intact.[6]

Both groups contended for the support of Lincoln and federal officials in New Orleans. Military governor Shepley authorized the Free State group's registry of voters, though he took no other action, while Banks, although preoccupied with organizing his command, backed the organization's moderate wing. The Conservative Unionists, for their part, sent a delegation to Washington in late May to solicit Lincoln's backing for their plan. Seeking from the federal government "a full recognition of all the rights of the State, as they existed previous to the passage of an act of secession, upon the principle of the existence of the State Constitution unimpaired," and avowing that "under this constitution the State wishes to return to its full allegiance, in the enjoyment of all rights and privileges exercised by the other states under the Federal Constitution," the delegates asked Lincoln to order an election, "in conformity with the constitution and laws of the State," in early November for state and federal officials.

In mid-June, Lincoln firmly but diplomatically declined the request. Since receiving it, he explained, he had received "reliable information . . . that a respectable portion of the Louisiana people desire to amend their State constitution, and contemplate holding a convention for that object. This fact alone, as it seems to me, is a sufficient reason why the general government should not give the committal you seek, to the existing State constitution." Lincoln's refusal to support the Conservative Unionists may not have amounted to an unequivocal endorsement of the Free State organization, but the language of his response—citing the Free State organization's intent to amend (actually rewrite) the constitution, clearly to abolish slavery—left little doubt where he stood. With the campaigns against Vicksburg and Port Hudson intensifying, moreover, Lincoln perhaps tried to soften the blow by invoking military necessity, remarking that an endorsement of Louisiana's existing (proslavery) constitution would not help military operations and might "be so used as to embarrass them." Yet Lincoln also decided against even more conciliatory language that Secretary of State William H. Seward had suggested. Presented with contrasting proposals for Louisiana's reconstruction, Lincoln endorsed, however carefully, the one that included abolishing slavery. His endorsement did not bring harmony to the Free State organization, as future events would show, but in late June 1863 these matters took a backseat to military affairs.[7]

II

Even as Lincoln navigated the complexities of reconstruction politics in Congress and the southern states during the first half of 1863, he faced the dual challenges of defending his administration's conduct of the war and maintaining public support for it. These difficulties were nothing new for Lincoln, but now added to them was the burden of justifying his emancipation policy against criticism from northern Democrats and even some Republicans. This criticism assumed special salience in light of the dismal military situation and the severe drubbing Republicans had endured in the fall 1862 elections. Aware of the significance of public opinion in a democracy, Lincoln came to realize that he needed to more actively shape northern perceptions of the war. No longer just about union, or even the fate of democratic government, the war would come to assume a transcendent meaning.

Throughout 1863, Lincoln's defense of the war and of his emancipation policy went hand-in-hand with his efforts to deflect calls for a negotiated settlement as a means of restoring the Union. It was obvious that any negotiated settlement, or even temporary cease-fire, would have to include at least a suspension of the Emancipation Proclamation, an eventuality as objectionable to Lincoln as was the proclamation itself to Confederates. Lincoln's defense of emancipation, in turn, further contributed to his broadened understanding of reconstruction. While restoring the national authority over the seceded states always remained central to Lincoln's vision, reconstruction would increasingly entail a new conception of the place of black people in American society. During his career, Lincoln had tread carefully through the minefield of racial politics, but from 1863 on he began to ascribe a new meaning to American democracy.

Criticism of the war and calls for negotiations came from both ends of the northern political spectrum. Although the rationale for the Emancipation Proclamation included preempting European intervention or recognition of the Confederacy, the proclamation did not end these possibilities. In early 1863, the fervently antislavery but equally eccentric newspaper editor Horace Greeley, among the most vociferous proponents of emancipation, had concluded that the war was lost and publicly called for European mediation. Greeley traveled to Washington to promote an informal proposal from French emperor Napoleon III, but his efforts were so clumsy that they backfired, and nothing came of them. Meanwhile, northern Democratic criticism of the war intensified. Opposition was especially keen in New York City and the southern portions of Ohio, Indiana, and Illinois. The legislatures of the latter two states passed resolutions advocating a cease-fire and peace conference, and Ohio witnessed the notorious military arrest and imprisonment of Peace Democrat Clement Vallandigham, whom Lincoln eventually banished to the Confederacy.[8]

Within this context, Lincoln's defense of emancipation evolved along two distinct but complementary paths. First, Lincoln justified emancipation in historical and idealistic terms. Abolishing slavery would fulfill the principles of the American Revolution and the promise of the American experiment in freedom and democratic government, while bringing to fruition the liberation of mankind and the inexorable march of human progress. As Lincoln had insisted in his message to the special congressional session of July 1861, well before the Emancipation Proclamation, the war was "a struggle for maintaining in the world, that form, and substance of government, whose leading object is, to elevate the condition of men—to lift artificial weights from all shoulders—to clear the paths of laudable pursuit for all—to afford all, an unfettered start, and a fair chance, in the race of life." Notwithstanding the limitations of Lincoln's racial thought before 1863, his articulation of these ideals and insistence on their universality eventually rendered impossible efforts to deny their applicability to black people.[9]

Lincoln amplified these themes in several public letters during this period, including one in January 1863 to the workingmen of Manchester, England. This letter was in response to their resolutions praising the Emancipation Proclamation despite the devastation the Union blockade had caused to the English textile industry. "I know and deeply deplore the sufferings which the workingmen at Manchester and in all Europe are called to endure in this crisis," Lincoln noted. Such sufferings resulted from the European powers' sympathy for "the attempt to overthrow this government, which was built upon the foundation of human rights, and to substitute for it one which should rest exclusively on the basis of human slavery." Under such circumstances, he deemed the workingmen's "decisive utterance upon the question as an instance of sublime Christian heroism which has not been surpassed in any age or in any country." Indeed, it was "an energetic and reinspiring assurance of the inherent power of truth and of the ultimate and universal triumph of justice, humanity, and freedom." The letter also included unmistakable appeals to the British government to refrain from supporting the Confederacy, on the basis of these broad, humanitarian principles.[10]

At the same time, Lincoln also began forging a more pragmatic defense of the proclamation. During the next two years, he would argue in increasingly forceful language that the assistance and support of black Americans—northerners, former slaves freed during the war, and even those still enslaved within the Confederacy—were essential to the Union war effort. Just as Lincoln justified the Emancipation Proclamation as a necessary measure for suppressing rebellion, he likewise refused to rescind it on the grounds that were he to do so, and thus renege on the promise of freedom, black people would abandon the Union cause, dealing the war effort a crippling blow. Much has been made of the constitutional, political, and even diplomatic factors that convinced Lincoln to issue and defend the proclamation, but this feature of his argument has perhaps been underappreciated. Lincoln's reasoning shortchanged black Americans' commitment to the Union cause, to which they had rallied even before the proclamation, though with some reservations. Yet it also recognized black people as political subjects who possessed a will and agency of their own.

This pragmatic defense of emancipation coincided with Lincoln's support for enlisting black men into the US military. Although Lincoln had expressed doubts on black enlistment, even after issuing the proclamation, once he decided on the matter he endorsed it wholeheartedly. In a series of letters to military commanders and political leaders in early 1863, Lincoln began laying out the argument that black troops were critical to the war effort and that black men could not be expected to enlist if the federal government were to rescind emancipation. Most of these letters were private communications not intended for public consumption, but they unequivocally encouraged their recipients to employ black troops or commended them for having done so. They also previewed arguments Lincoln soon began making publicly and would make for the remainder of the war. "The colored population is the great *available* and yet *unavailed of,* force for restoring the Union," he remarked to Andrew Johnson. "The bare sight of fifty thousand armed, and drilled black soldiers on the banks of the Mississippi, would end the rebellion at once. And who doubts that we can present that sight, if we but take hold in earnest?" Hyperbole notwithstanding, black military service indeed became essential to Union success and enabled Lincoln to maintain his emancipation policy on practical grounds, if no other. Yet it also became integral to his incorporating black freedom into the process of reconstruction.[11]

The near-simultaneous Union victories at Gettysburg and Vicksburg in early July, which together proved to be a major turning point in the war, further altered the contest over public opinion. Whereas many northerners had previously advocated a cease-fire owing to Union weakness, they now envisioned a cessation of hostilities from a position of strength. Some of Lincoln's own supporters over-optimistically anticipated the war's imminent end, while Democrats intensified their charge that Confederates might now be amenable to talks over restoring the Union—if only Lincoln would drop his misguided emancipation policy. Lincoln redoubled his efforts in kind, rejecting negotiations with the Confederacy on any basis other than the complete restoration of the Union and the abolition of slavery, even if gradual. For the rest of the war, Lincoln walked a fine line between urging the northern public on to total victory while remaining open to Confederate overtures, though on his terms.

No sooner had news of the dual Union victories arrived in Washington than Lincoln reminded northerners of the war's broader meaning. Responding to a serenade, he offered impromptu remarks that resembled the Gettysburg Address enough to suggest he had already been carefully considering the themes it would contain. "How long ago is it?" he asked rhetorically, "—eighty odd years—since on the Fourth of July for the first time in the history of the world a nation by its representatives, assembled and declared as a self-evident truth that 'all men are created equal.'" Twice more during his brief comments, Lincoln affirmed that the Union fought in defense of that principle, and the Confederacy to overturn it.[12]

Approximately one week later, in mid-July, Lincoln indicated his willingness to talk to Confederate leaders—but only if they would agree to reunion and emancipation. In a private White House meeting, Lincoln approved of a letter written in his presence by James R. Gilmore to North Carolina governor Zebulon B. Vance, responding to remarks Vance purportedly made (not to Gilmore but to an inter-mediary) admitting that the Confederate cause was lost and slavery was dead, and pledging to use his influence "to bring about any reunion that would admit the South on terms of perfect equality with the North." In response, Gilmore attested to Lincoln's hopes "for the restoration of peace between the States, and for a reunion of all the States on the basis of the abolition of slavery,—the bone we are fighting over,—and the full reinstatement of every Confeder-ate citizen in all the rights of citizenship in our common country." Were these points agreed to, Gilmore continued, Lincoln would gladly "receive overtures from any man, or body of men, who have authority to control the armies of the Confederacy," and he and the US Congress "will be found very liberal on all collateral points that may come up in the settlement." Although a fledgling but ill-fated peace movement was emerging in North Carolina that Lincoln hoped to exploit, and while he repeatedly offered generous capitula-tion terms to Confederates for the remainder of the war, he would insist time and again that restoration of the Union not come at the cost of emancipation.[13]

During this period, Lincoln most systematically integrated his defense of emancipation, rejection of negotiations, and affirmation of the black contribution to the Union war effort in his open letter to James C. Conkling, a staunch Republican and long-time friend from Springfield, Illinois. Read before a large Union rally in Lincoln's adopted hometown in early September, the letter addressed neither Conkling nor Republicans but rather Lincoln's northern opponents. And although eschewing partisanship, it offered an unabashed apolo-gia of his administration's conduct of the war while further conjoin-ing black freedom and Union victory. Lincoln began by asserting that peace was achievable only through the rebellion's suppression, its success, or compromise. His position on the first two was obvious, and he insisted that any compromise "embracing the maintenance of the Union" was impossible. Downplaying the effects of southern Unionism and various manifestations of Confederate discontent, Lincoln reasoned that so long as those who controlled the Confeder-ate military power refused to compromise, there could be none. He assured his audience that "no word or intimation, from that rebel army, or from any of the men controlling it, in relation to any peace compromise" had ever come to his knowledge, and any allegations to the contrary were "deceptive and groundless."

If these words even hinted at compromise, Lincoln's defense of emancipation dispelled any such notion, and he moved to the crux of the matter. "But, to be plain," he told his opponents, "you are dissatisfied with me about the negro." He emphasized his differences with them by asserting, perhaps not entirely fairly: "I certainly wish that all men could be free, while I suppose you do not." He defended the Emancipation Proclamation as constitutional and legal, and, responding to the charge that it was bad policy, he countered that the Union had fought for a year and a half before attacking slavery and had made little progress, whereas it had made much since. Why would the original policy work any better now? In fact, some Union commanders, neither abolitionist nor Republican, believed that "the emancipation policy, and the use of colored troops, constitute the heaviest blow yet dealt to the rebellion." Lincoln pointed out the contradiction of distinguishing between a war for Union and one for freedom when black men were involved in the conflict, observing: "You say you will not fight to free negroes. Some of them seem willing to fight for you; but, no matter. Fight you, then, exclusively to save the Union." Still, Lincoln admitted that his emancipation policy had been undertaken primarily to suppress the rebellion, and he allowed that once that goal had been achieved, "it will be an apt time, then, for you to declare you will not fight to free negroes."

Having conceded ground for the sake of argument, Lincoln seized it right back. He again employed his pragmatic defense of emancipation and black enlistment, but this time to explore what these things meant to black people themselves. As both civilians and soldiers, they could either help or weaken the Union cause. There was no middle ground. "But negroes, like other people, act upon motives. Why should they do any thing for us," he asked rhetorically, "if we will do nothing for them?" He continued: "If they stake their lives for us, they must be prompted by the strongest motive—even the promise of freedom. And the promise being made, must be kept."

Lincoln may have framed this argument around narrow self-interest, but, to his credit, both his northern and southern opponents would have disputed the basic assumption that black people were (or are) simply "like other people." That, as Lincoln himself might have said, was the rub. Lincoln closed by reaffirming the historic significance of the Union cause and the black contribution to it. Union victory, once achieved, would prove that "among free men, there can be no successful appeal from the ballot to the bullet," he insisted. "And then, there will be some black men who can remember that, with silent tongue, and clenched teeth, and steady eye, and well-poised bayonet, they have helped mankind on to this great consummation." Lincoln was still far from embracing legal or political equality, or from endorsing what would later be known as "civil rights," but his language was indicative of an inexorable move toward that position.[14]

Lincoln's Conkling letter was but one of several documents issued during mid-1863 defending his administration's conduct of the war. Others included justifications for suspending the writ of habeas corpus and, following the New York City draft riots of mid-July, the draft. Public response to these letters was largely positive, and they helped galvanize northern support for the war. Yet Lincoln's most eloquent and, in the long run, most influential attempt to define the war generated the words for which he is best known—the Gettysburg Address, delivered in November at the dedication of the National Cemetery. Lincoln had long contemplated a statement on the war's transcendent meaning, to help Americans comprehend the death and suffering they were enduring, but he also crafted the address with the more immediate goal in mind of downplaying any armistice or negotiated settlement short of military victory. In dedicating the grounds, Lincoln observed, he and his listeners must also be "dedicated . . . to the unfinished work" for which the dead had given their lives and "to the great task remaining before us." That task was to defend a nation, and form of government, "conceived in Liberty, and dedicated to the proposition, that all men are created equal." As scholars have often noted, by invoking the Declaration of Independence, Lincoln was transforming the meaning of the war: from Union and the constitution to freedom and equality—even though Americans were barely beginning to fathom the consequences of that transformation. The war was a test, Lincoln believed, to determine "whether that nation, or any nation, so conceived and so dedicated, can long endure," and from that test, he famously proclaimed, the nation would not merely be preserved but would have "a new birth of freedom." The United States as a confederation of free and slaveholding states, in which only certain men and women were created equal, was dead, to be replaced by a modern nation-state, in which all would be. The war would continue, Lincoln pledged, not to restore but to reconstruct the Union.[15]

III

Lincoln's defense of emancipation led him to begin thinking seriously about incorporating black people into American society, if not necessarily as full citizens. Yet in the South, progress toward a mode of state restoration encompassing the abolition of slavery remained painfully slow. In Tennessee, the conservative Unionist attempt to displace military governor Andrew Johnson, combined with the federal inability to take Lookout Mountain until November, kept reconstruction on hold. Hopes had been raised with the Union capture of Chattanooga in early September, and Lincoln encouraged Johnson to organize a new state government and write a free-state constitution as quickly as possible. "Get emancipation into your new State government—Constitution—and there will be no such word as fail for your case," he advised. The Union debacle later that month at Chickamauga, however, belied Lincoln's optimism for a speedy reconstruction of Tennessee.[16]

Events in Arkansas, Missouri, and Louisiana also brought both hope and disappointment. Union victories in early 1862 had raised the possibility of restoring Arkansas, but no further military or political progress was made for the rest of the year, and the entire state was included in the Emancipation Proclamation. In July 1863, however, William K. Sebastian, a former US Senator who resigned when Arkansas seceded, indicated a willingness to resume his seat, prompting Lincoln to write to General Stephan A. Hurlbut, the Union commander in Memphis, where Sebastian was residing. Lincoln conceded that the Senate must decide on seating Sebastian, but he hoped to link his seating, and Arkansas's readmission, to the abolition of slavery. Insisting that the proclamation applied to Arkansas and would not be retracted, Lincoln suggested that gradual emancipation—though beginning immediately—would be acceptable. "Those who shall have tasted actual freedom I believe can never be slaves, or quasi slaves again," Lincoln noted. "For the rest, I believe some plan, substantially being gradual emancipation, would be better for both white and black. . . . If Senator Sebastian could come with something of this sort from Arkansas, I at least should take great interest in his case; and I believe a single individual will have scarcely done the world so great a service." Sebastian evidently declined Lincoln's proposal, and the initiative died. Any disappointment Lincoln may have felt would have been tempered by his having avoided the troubling possibility of slaves whom the proclamation had declared free remaining in bondage. Moreover, Lincoln had reaffirmed the abolition of slavery as a fundamental condition for state readmission.[17]

Lincoln's Arkansas proposal was prompted in part by events in neighboring Missouri, one of the four loyal slave states. Although border-state emancipation was no longer as critical to the war effort as it had been, it remained essential to the overall campaign to abolish slavery. Missouri had witnessed, in addition to violent partisan warfare, bitter strife between civilian and military authorities and between radical and conservative Unionists, strife that Lincoln had repeatedly tried but failed to resolve. Despite their infighting, Missouri Unionists by summer 1863 were holding a constitutional convention to consider abolishing slavery. Commenting on the convention in late June, Lincoln indicated he would endorse just about any legitimate abolition plan. "I have very earnestly urged the slave-states to adopt emancipation," he noted to the Union military commander in Missouri, "and it ought to be, and is an object with me not to overthrow, or thwart what any of them may in good faith do, to that end." However, the convention soon thereafter adopted a gradual emancipation plan that would not begin until 1870, and even then would never free most adult slaves. Lincoln was clearly disappointed in the Missouri plan. Indeed, it was in his letter to Hurlbut—proposing a gradual plan for Arkansas that would begin immediately—that he expressed his dismay. "The Missouri plan, recently adopted, I do not object to on account of the time for *ending* the institution; but I am sorry the *beginning* should have been postponed for seven years, leaving all that time to agitate for the repeal of the whole thing," he observed. "It should begin at once, giving at least the new-born, a vested interest in freedom, which could not be taken away." The plan was never implemented, but this was of little comfort to Lincoln, and Missouri affairs continued to vex him for the remainder of his presidency.[18]

As though these reconstruction efforts were not frustrating enough, those in Louisiana produced what one historian has called a "comedy of errors." After Lincoln had endorsed the Free State organization over the proslavery Conservative Unionists in June, he expected the plan for a registry of loyal citizens and constitutional convention to move forward. Those expectations were augmented in early August when military governor Shepley informed Lincoln that arrangements were being made for the proposed registry. They did not work out as planned, however, causing Lincoln to write a series of letters during the next several months to military commander Nathaniel P. Banks in which he expressed his vision for, and frustration over, reconstruction in Louisiana.[19]

Lincoln's letter of early August characteristically offered suggestions rather than directives. "While I very well know what I would be glad for Louisiana to do, it is quite a different thing for me to assume direction of the matter." Endorsing the registry of voters, he assured Banks that he "would be glad for [Louisiana] to make a new Constitution recognizing the emancipation proclamation, and adopting emancipation in those parts of the state to which the proclamation does not apply." He reaffirmed, as he often did, that the proclamation would not be retracted and no person freed by it (or by act of Congress) would be reenslaved. Lincoln then addressed the social and economic status of (formerly enslaved) plantation laborers, especially those excluded from the proclamation. He likely did so because Banks earlier that year had issued labor regulations for Union-occupied Louisiana that slavery's opponents criticized as too harsh and its defenders as too lenient. "And while she [Louisiana] is at it, I think it would not be objectionable for her to adopt some practical system by which the two races could gradually live themselves out of their old relation to each other, and both come out better prepared for the new," he noted. "Education for young blacks should be included in the plan. After all, the power, or element, of 'contract' may be sufficient for this probationary period; and, by it's simplicity, and flexibility, may be the better." Lincoln thus expressed his belief that former slaveholders and former slaves would be able to come to terms on mutually agreeable labor arrangements to replace slavery, a viewpoint he would increasingly come to question over the next year. And while noting that Congress would judge the qualifications of members-elect, Lincoln hinted that a government based on the principles he outlined would find approval in Washington. "I think the thing should be pushed forward," he urged Banks, "so that if possible, it's mature work may reach here by the meeting of Congress."[20]

This was certainly an ambitious timetable. During the previous fifteen months, some progress had been made toward Louisiana reconstruction. Congressional elections had been held and a fledgling free-labor system had begun to take shape. Lincoln now hoped that a new constitution would be written, a new state government organized, and a new labor system largely in place by the time Congress convened in early December, a mere four months hence. Banks himself saw no problem, assuring Lincoln in early September that Louisiana could be restored to the Union by year's end. Yet the plan was as unrealistic as it was ambitious, and it quickly unraveled. Banks turned his attention to military operations in Texas and was absent for much of the fall, leaving political affairs to Shepley and the Free State organization. The registration of voters bogged down, factionalism between Free-State radicals and moderates intensified, and the Conservative Unionists did their best to obstruct a reconstruction process from which they were largely excluded. Worse still, neither Lincoln's letter to Banks nor Secretary of War Edwin M. Stanton's subsequent instructions to Shepley clearly specified who was to take charge of the process or how it was to proceed.

Finding little progress and much bickering by late October, Lincoln again wrote to Banks, this time uncharacteristically admitting the situation "disappoints me bitterly." Without assigning blame, he urged the parties involved to avoid further delay. Shepley and the Free State leaders, Lincoln insisted, must "go to work and give me a tangible nucleus which the remainder of the State may rally around as fast as it can, and which I can at once recognize and sustain as the true State government." He encouraged Banks and everyone under his command to provide all the support they could, but this initiative had to be the work of "the loyal element"—which for Lincoln meant not just Unionists but advocates of emancipation. "If a few professedly loyal men shall draw the disloyal about them, and colorably set up a State government, repudiating the emancipation proclamation, and reestablishing slavery," he cautioned, "I can not recognize or sustain their work. I should fall powerless in the attempt. This government, in such an attitude," he advised, using familiar language, "would be a house divided against itself." Again addressing the former slaves' status, Lincoln indicated his approval were the state government, "acting in harmony with [the federal] government, and consistently with general freedom, . . . to adopt a reasonable temporary arrangement, in relation to the landless and homeless freed people." But, he emphasized, "my word is out to be *for* and not *against* them on the question of their permanent freedom."[21]

Banks was understandably mortified after reading this letter in early December. He hastily replied that he had not been clearly authorized to carry out Lincoln's wishes and thus could not be held responsible for failing to do so. "Had the organization of a *free* state in Louisiana been committed to me under general instructions only, it would have been complete before this day," he insisted, displaying his usual overstatement. "It can be effected now in sixty days—let me say, even in *thirty* days, if necessary." Lincoln may have been unrealistic, but Banks was arguably delusional.[22]

Lincoln responded in late December, after he had already issued his Proclamation of Amnesty and Reconstruction (of which he made no mention). He attempted to assuage Banks's hurt feelings by assuming virtually all the blame for the Louisiana situation. To prevent any future confusion, Lincoln used the word "master" no less than four times in placing Banks unequivocally in charge of the state's reconstruction: "I now distinctly tell you that you are master of all, and that I wish you to take the case as you find it, and give us a free-state reorganization of Louisiana, in the shortest possible time." Banks's political duties were not to take priority over military matters; neither was he expected "to throw away available work already done for re-construction." Still, responsibility for restoring a seceded state to the Union with slavery abolished now rested firmly on his shoulders. Thirteen months after having eschewed placing reconstruction under "our military and quasi-military, authorities" in Louisiana, Lincoln was doing just that, but the strategy of urging local Unionists to take the initiative with the support of military officials had failed. Lincoln's "Louisiana experiment" would assume increasing significance throughout 1864 and for the remainder of the war, as Banks oversaw creation of a free-state government. But if Banks were now "master of all" in Louisiana, he would be operating within the parameters of Lincoln's own formal reconstruction plan.[23]

IV

Despite Lincoln's efforts to keep northerners "dedicated" to the goal of victory, recent Union military success—including Lookout Mountain in November, securing eastern Tennessee—led by late 1863 to general expectation of a formal presidential statement on reconstruction. Lincoln himself realized that the Union's brightening military prospects, along with the unsettled state of affairs in Louisiana and Tennessee, increasing Confederate discontent, and Congress's failure to enact reconstruction legislation, necessitated a presidential initiative. It was no secret by late fall that Lincoln was drafting such a plan. The result was the Proclamation of Amnesty and Reconstruction, better known as the "ten-percent plan," issued on December 8 as part of Lincoln's annual message to Congress. It would be difficult to overstate the importance of this document to understanding Lincoln and reconstruction.[24]

There is a tendency among scholars to view the plan as a major departure in Lincoln's presidency. Whereas Lincoln had previously focused almost exclusively on the war, he now recognized the need for an official reconstruction policy. While the ten-percent plan must indeed be seen as something of a new departure, it is also true that almost everything he had done since the start of the war was geared toward reconstructing the Union, even if his definition of reconstruction now included emancipation. The ten-percent plan must therefore be seen within the broader continuities of Lincoln's approach to reconstruction. And yet, the ten-percent plan did mark a distinct break, one that coincided with the transformation of the war. Just as emancipation redefined the war, it also redefined reconstruction—from restoring federal authority over the seceded states to the fundamental remaking of southern slave society. The ten-percent plan was a major departure not because Lincoln was finally turning his attention to reconstruction, but because he was formally incorporating emancipation into the process of reconstruction.

As its formal title makes clear, Lincoln's plan rested on the principle of the presidential pardon or amnesty. Invoking the constitutional provision and congressional laws granting him that power, Lincoln would grant full pardon to any person who had participated "directly or by implication" in the rebellion, "with restoration of all rights of property, except as to slaves," provided that said person swore and kept inviolate an oath to uphold the constitution and to abide by all wartime measures concerning slavery. The pardon was thus made contingent on pledging future loyalty and accepting emancipation. (Certain classes of persons were excluded, mostly high-ranking Confederate officials and those who had mistreated Union prisoners of war.) For each seceded state, once a number of persons equivalent to one-tenth of the votes cast in the 1860 presidential election had taken the oath, then those who had taken the oath, and who had been qualified voters in the state just before secession, "and excluding all others," could "re-establish a State government which shall be republican, and in no wise contravening said oath, [and] such shall be recognized as the true government of the State." By insisting that the new state governments be "republican" in nature and "in no wise contravening said oath," Lincoln was requiring the seceded states, however implicitly, to abolish slavery in order to be restored to the Union.

Beyond the abolition of slavery, the plan did not require the states to address the political and legal rights of the former slaves. It did not even mention that topic. Lincoln indicated, however, that he would not object—which was often his way of saying he favored something—"to any provision which may be adopted by such State government in relation to the freed people of such State, which shall recognize and declare their permanent freedom, provide for their education, and may yet be consistent, as a temporary arrangement, with their present condition as a laboring, landless, and homeless class." Other than providing for emancipation and its immediate consequences, no further changes were demanded of the states: their names, boundaries, subdivisions, constitutions, and laws could otherwise remain unaltered. The plan was intended for the seceded states only and had no applicability to the loyal states, and Lincoln affirmed congressional input by explicitly recognizing that Congress would judge the qualifications of members-elect from reconstructed states. Finally, Lincoln demonstrated his flexibility by declaring that his plan constituted "a mode" of restoring federal authority in the South, and that "it must not be understood that no other possible mode would be acceptable."

In elaborating on the plan in his annual message, Lincoln focused on three issues: the pardoning power, the "temporary arrangement" for the freed people, and the plan's political implications. The first received by far the fullest explication. Lincoln began by observing that the constitution gives the president "absolute discretion" in pardoning and that the proposed oath was voluntary. He then invoked the constitutional provision that the federal government guarantee a "republican" form of government for the states, which, he insisted, was intended for instances where a state's loyal element "may be too feeble for an opposite and hostile element external to, or even within the State; and such are precisely the cases with which we are now dealing." It would be "simply absurd" to attempt to (re)establish a state government without distinguishing between the loyal and hostile elements and without specifying that only the former exercise power. "There must be a test by which to separate the opposing elements, so as to build only from the sound," Lincoln reasoned, "and that test is a sufficiently liberal one, which accepts as sound whoever will make a sworn recantation of his former unsoundness." In short, the presidential pardon, requiring an oath of future loyalty, could be used to rebuild a political community.

But if the pardon demanded loyalty to the constitution, Lincoln rhetorically asked, why must it also require acceptance of measures concerning slavery? Here Lincoln again employed his pragmatic argument: these measures had been adopted of necessity to suppress the rebellion, and "to give them their fullest effect, there had to be a pledge for their maintenance." Because the measures had greatly assisted the Union war effort and would likely do so in the future, Lincoln continued, "to now abandon them would be not only to relinquish a lever of power, but would also be a cruel and an astounding breach of faith." He restated his familiar refrain that the Emancipation Proclamation would be neither modified nor retracted and no person freed during the war would be reenslaved. "For these and other reasons it is thought best that support of these measures shall be included in the oath; and it is believed the Executive may lawfully claim it in return for pardon and restoration of forfeited rights, which he has clear constitutional power to withhold altogether, or grant upon the terms which he shall deem wisest for the public interest." Lincoln granted, though, that this part of the oath could be modified or voided by Congress or the Supreme Court.

Lincoln's acquiescence to any "temporary arrangement" the new state governments might adopt concerning the former slaves was made, as he put it, "with the view of possibly modifying the confusion and destitution which must, at best, attend all classes by a total revolution of labor throughout whole States." By late 1863 various free-labor arrangements had emerged in the Union-occupied South that were both cause and effect of much conflict on farms and plantations. Whereas Lincoln had previously indicated a willingness to countenance apprenticeship—whereby former slaves would be bound to work for a set number of years or until they had reached a certain age—or other arrangements that defined former slaves as quasi-free laborers, his words also demonstrate the serious thought he was already devoting to the "total revolution of labor" emancipation would entail. His insisting that such arrangements be reasonable and temporary, however imprecise those terms, probably owed more to his moderate temperament than to callousness over the former slaves' welfare. Even as he recognized, moreover, that white southerners might more readily abandon the war effort "if, to this extent, this vital matter be left to themselves," he also insisted that "no power of the national Executive to prevent an abuse is abridged by the proposition." Thus, Lincoln offered white southerners considerable latitude in determining the region's new labor system as an inducement to return to the Union, but he did not grant them carte blanche. And over the coming months, he would reconsider both the wide discretion he was granting them and the prospects for a speedy transformation of the South's labor system.

Lincoln closed by addressing the plan's broader political implications. Why even issue a proclamation now on the subject, he again asked rhetorically, when opinions differed on whether "the step might be delayed too long or be taken too soon"? In effect, he responded that conditions in some of the seceded states appeared conducive to reconstruction but for want of a clear plan: in certain instances southern Unionists disagreed on how to proceed, in others they agreed but hesitated lest the federal government reject their plan. Thus, Lincoln offered his proposal both as "a rallying point" and to reassure potential Unionists that their efforts would meet with approval. "This may bring them to act sooner than they otherwise would." To the objection that the plan might prematurely commit him on certain questions best left to the future, Lincoln responded that it had been crafted so as to avoid this predicament. "Saying that reconstruction will be accepted if presented in a specified way," he avowed, "it is not said it will never be accepted in any other way." Lincoln then concluded by applauding the recent efforts of the border states to abolish slavery and urging Congress to provide them the necessary assistance, and by reminding the nation that reconstruction ultimately depended on "the war power," which alone could give southern loyalists the confidence that secessionists would not again overwhelm them. "Until that confidence shall be established, little can be done anywhere for what is called reconstruction."

Lincoln's plan contained features pleasing to both conservative and radical Republicans. For conservatives, the plan considered secession the work of individuals requiring pardon rather than of states, which remained intact; it rejected territorialization and other similar ideas; and it conceded the abstract possibility of either Congress or the Supreme Court overturning the Emancipation Proclamation even as it went a long way toward making emancipation irreversible. It also eschewed black suffrage or other measures regarding racial equality; it adhered to states rights by allowing the southern states to adopt "temporary arrangement[s]" regarding the former slaves; and its restoration of property rights seemed to leave little room for confiscation. In a larger sense, the plan's language was conciliatory, if firm; it based loyalty on future rather than on past acts; and it dealt with reconstruction as a practical and not a theoretical problem, the latter being identified with the radical approach. And, as Michael Vorenberg has noted, the plan did not call for an amendment to the US constitution abolishing slavery, as some of Lincoln's advisers had recommended, it did not require the seceded states to abolish slavery immediately, and it made no provision for slavery in the border states. For radicals, the plan explicitly held that the seceded state governments had been "subverted"; it affirmed the reliance on military power and thus favored conquest over conciliation; it asserted executive oversight to prevent "abuse" while allowing for temporary labor arrangements; and it left open the possibility of more extensive changes. Perhaps most importantly, the plan required all white southerners to take the oath in order to participate in creating new state governments, and it made accepting emancipation a fundamental condition of both individual pardon and state restoration.

Contemporaries debated, as have scholars, the leniency of Lincoln's plan toward white southerners. Proponents of this characterization have focused much attention on basing the presidential pardon—and thus the ability to participate in reconstruction—on a pledge of future loyalty rather than on past actions, and on requiring only ten percent of a state's voters to take the oath in order to begin reconstruction. The alternative to the pledge of future loyalty was the "ironclad oath," which required a person to swear to never having voluntarily aided the Confederacy and would have barred the large majority of white southern men. It is likely that one-tenth of the white male population in most of the Confederate states might have met this requirement, but in the confused conditions of the wartime South, fulfilling it would have been nearly impossible. Lincoln would have opposed such a policy in principle, but it also contradicted his practical goal of inducing Confederates to resume their loyalty to the Union. The ironclad oath would become increasingly identified with Radical Republicans and with southern Unionists in their postwar political battles with former Confederates. For now, Lincoln would accept as "sound" anyone who made "a sworn recantation of his former unsoundness."

Moreover, even Lincoln's supporters doubted the wisdom of founding governments on such a small minority. While these governments could not legitimately claim to represent "the people" of the states, Lincoln hoped to create "a rallying point," or, as he had put it to Nathaniel Banks, "a tangible nucleus," that, by starting small, might appear to gain momentum as it attracted adherents. Inducing even one tenth of the white southern population to renounce its Confederate allegiance in the midst of war would have been a considerable achievement. The plan was lenient to the white South, but a more accurate characterization might be to see it as a realistic assessment of what was possible under the circumstances. It was justice tempered by both realism and mercy.

Yet whatever its merits, the ten-percent plan was somewhat misguided. Neither a blueprint for postwar reconstruction nor a tactic for winning the war, it is perhaps best seen as a means of achieving what Lincoln had always maintained was the war's main objective: restoring the national authority over the seceded states. Following from this "restorationist" thinking, the plan could hardly have initiated a genuine reintegration of the seceded states into the Union against widespread white opposition. Any new governments Lincoln's plan might create—even were they to write new constitutions abolishing slavery and return members to Congress—would still face the challenge of asserting their authority over the large majority of those states' white populations, which, for all the suffering they had endured, were still determined to resist. Lincoln's plan seemed to assume that competing, roughly equivalent elements were vying for power in the seceded states, and that the Union strategy was to enable the "sound" element to succeed. But this was not the case. Whatever internal opposition it generated, the Confederacy for the most part managed to maintain broad popular support. New governments would eventually be created in several states under Lincoln's plan, but none ever established its legitimacy with the white population at large. Lincoln may have abandoned his original conception of secession as the work of a political minority, but the ten-percent plan did not solve the problem of how—short of black suffrage, a solution some Radical Republicans were coming to advocate—to reconstruct states in opposition to their white populations.

Nonetheless, the plan broke new ground. Emancipation was now a fundamental condition of both the reorganization of states and the political rehabilitation of individuals. Lincoln's plan did not end northern conservative calls for retracting the Emancipation Proclamation or for a cease-fire, neither did it preclude the possibility of Confederates suing for peace on the basis of preserving slavery. But it dictated that state readmission would require the effective elimination of slavery, though not specifying how that were to be done. In a strictly technical sense, the plan reflected Lincoln's constitutional conservatism. Rather than explicitly calling for the seceded states to abolish slavery, the plan directed that they comply with all proclamations and laws concerning it. Just as the federal government under the constitution was powerless to act against slavery in the states (other than in suppressing rebellion), it likewise could not explicitly mandate that a state formally abolish slavery. The federal government could, by contrast, require a new state government and constitution—being created by the loyal element within a state engaged in rebellion against the United States—to comply with all measures concerning slavery that had been instituted in suppressing rebellion. Lincoln's plan was thus as direct and explicit an order as the federal government could possibly give under the constitution to a state to abolish slavery. In however veiled a manner, the plan made evident—as a matter of policy—the distinction between federal wartime emancipation measures and the abolition of slavery as an institution. In doing so, it also helped to make the constitutional abolition of slavery a politically viable position for Republicans in 1864.

In dealing with individuals, the plan decreed that all white southerners would have to take an oath to abide by emancipation in order to participate in the reconstruction process. This provision rankled many Unionists, who would have to take the same oath as would Confederates, but Lincoln was announcing that Unionism now required not only loyalty but also accepting emancipation. The plan would thus prevent slavery's rear-guard defenders from rejoining the Union in hopes of preserving slavery. Whereas the Emancipation Proclamation had defined out of existence the concept of loyal slaveholders within the Confederacy, the ten-percent plan equated loyalty for *all* white persons in the seceded states—not just slaveholders—with consenting to emancipation.

Lincoln's Proclamation of Amnesty and Reconstruction would have a checkered history. Requiring no specific congressional action, it received none. It facilitated the creation of new governments in several Confederate states, but only Louisiana's had any appreciable historical significance. And while the last public address Lincoln ever delivered was a defense of that Louisiana government, the fate of his reconstruction plan remains one of history's great what-ifs. Nonetheless, prior to passage of the Thirteenth Amendment in 1865, which was hardly a given, it was unclear whether the seceded states would be compelled to abolish slavery as a condition of their readmission to the Union. The ten-percent plan was Lincoln's announcement, however indirect, that they would be. Perhaps most importantly, by formally linking together the eventual abolition of slavery and the restoration of the seceded states to the Union, the ten-percent plan would also bring the *restorationist* and the genuinely *reconstructionist* dimensions of Lincoln's approach to reconstruction increasingly into conflict.

CHAPTER THREE

WAR, RECONSTRUCTION,
AND REELECTION
(December 1863–November 1864)

As had been true with the Emancipation Proclamation a year earlier, implementing the ten-percent plan throughout 1864 raised as many issues as it settled. Lincoln provided only basic guidelines for reconstructing the seceded states, making conflict virtually inevitable. Although new governments in the seceded states, and the restoration of those states to the Union, would be predicated on abolishing slavery, debate over the implications of emancipation was only beginning. The lenient loyalty oath designed to rehabilitate former Confederates provoked rather than prevented disagreements between them and Unionists, and among Unionists themselves. Lincoln tried to steer clear of these quarrels, yet they reflected the larger incompatibility between the restorationist and reconstructionist dimensions of his own approach to reconstruction. Issues pertinent to the remaking of southern society—which inevitably followed from the abolition of slavery—made the timely state restoration that Lincoln had hoped for all but impossible.

These difficulties contributed to the growing rift between Lincoln and congressional Republicans, the Radicals especially, over reconstruction. Having remained mostly latent since the war's start, political conflict manifested itself in the summer controversy over the Wade-Davis bill, the congressional alternative to the ten-percent plan that would have brought far-reaching change to the seceded states as the price of readmission. Although scholars debate whether the Wade-Davis imbroglio reflected genuine divisions between Lincoln and congressional Republicans, their contrasting reconstruction plans emanated from very different visions of the war and its consequences. Subsequent developments would reduce the dispute's significance, but at the time it loomed large, especially with the failure of the House of Representatives to approve a constitutional amendment abolishing slavery. Adoption of the Thirteenth Amendment was hardly inevitable, despite the emerging Republican consensus on the need to abolish slavery definitively through constitutional means. Consequently, tensions between Lincoln and congressional Republicans over reconstruction intensified.

The Wade-Davis dispute further heightened sentiment among many Republicans to replace Lincoln as the party's nominee in the fall presidential election. Compounding this threat to Lincoln's leadership was the criticism of his emancipation policy by northern Democrats and other conservatives, who continued to advocate retracting the Emancipation Proclamation and negotiating with the Confederacy. Despite what may have been a brief flirtation with these ideas, brought on by his grim reelection prospects, Lincoln ultimately rejected them. In doing so, he reaffirmed his commitment to emancipation and to the process, begun the previous year, of reconceptualizing black freedom.

Lincoln's political woes derived from the want of military success. The hopes raised in spring 1864 with the appointment of Ulysses S. Grant to command of the Union armies gave way to despair, as the Army of the Potomac—after suffering horrific losses during the Overland campaign of May and June—was reduced to laying siege to Petersburg. General William T. Sherman similarly remained bogged down outside Atlanta. By late August, expecting to lose the election, Lincoln composed his famous memorandum, but Union victories at Atlanta and elsewhere reversed his reelection prospects. Although debate over reconstruction was muted during the presidential campaign, reconstruction had clearly become inseparable from both the war and Lincoln's reelection. Indeed, even as Lincoln's reelection ensured Union military victory, postwar reconstruction went from prospective to imminent.

I

Working through military and civilian officials, Lincoln moved decisively in early 1864 to implement the ten-percent plan, precipitating what William C. Harris has called a "flurry of activity" in the southern states regarding reconstruction. Copies of the plan were distributed in Union-held areas; certificates of loyalty and "record books" were generated for registering oath-takers; and military commanders disseminated the plan among Confederate prisoners-of-war and soldiers. Southern Unionists seemed to be moving apace. Lincoln dispatched his secretary John Hay to assist restoration in northeast Florida. Efforts in eastern North Carolina were renewed after 1862's failure. And Lincoln's plan appeared to galvanize Unionism in northern Alabama, where Confederate discontent had previously spawned halting reconstruction efforts. Yet reconstruction in those states made little progress. The lack of sustained military success, Confederate raids, and generally unsettled conditions were all contributing factors, but most important was the plan's failure to attract popular support.[1]

Virginia appeared to offer potential success but yielded mixed results. The "Restored Government" of Francis H. Pierpont controlled limited territory at its start and even less after West Virginia's creation, but Lincoln's plan raised hopes for enhancing its legitimacy. Pierpont had recently converted to emancipation, and under his auspices a convention of only seventeen delegates met in Alexandria in early March, 1864, and adopted a constitution giving Virginia the distinction of being the first Confederate state to abolish slavery. The constitution provided no other rights to black people, and it became effective immediately, requiring no voter approval. Pierpont ordered May elections for county offices, which, despite attracting low turnout, gave the new constitution some legitimacy. Pierpont's success, however, was tempered by a bitter jurisdictional dispute with General Benjamin F. Butler, whose command included Norfolk and its environs, and whose repeated interference in civilian affairs undermined the Pierpont government. Lincoln had to tread carefully. However militarily incompetent, Butler was popular among both Radical Republicans and War Democrats, neither of whom Lincoln could afford to alienate. Yet Lincoln also had to sustain Pierpont and his own reconstruction policy. Not until early 1865, with his reelection secured, did Lincoln remove Butler. Virginia had abolished slavery, but its Unionist government could hardly be called representative.[2]

In Tennessee, Lincoln's plan did not induce Unionists to overcome their factional differences. Military governor Andrew Johnson had hesitated to move forward with reconstruction, ostensibly until eastern Tennessee had been liberated but also to keep his conservative opponents at bay. He authorized local rather than state elections for March, which was not quite in keeping with Lincoln's plan, and announced that only afterwards would a convention be held to abolish slavery. In a January speech he famously proclaimed "treason must be made odious and traitors must be punished," and he required a more stringent oath than Lincoln's for participating in the elections. Despite protests, Lincoln supported Johnson, but voter turnout was uneven. As they had done previously, moreover, conservative Unionists attempted to preempt Johnson, this time by calling for a convention to meet in April. Johnson and his supporters managed to attend the convention, which eventually adjourned after acrimonious but inconclusive debate over emancipation and Johnson's policy on Confederates. Later that month, east Tennessee Unionists held a mass meeting in Knoxville designed to rally support for a constitutional convention to abolish slavery, but they also condemned racial equality. Meanwhile, those local officials elected in March attempted to assume office but were hampered by guerilla raids. Although eastern Tennessee was finally cleared of Confederate forces by summer, widespread devastation and civilian suffering made political reorganization impossible, and no substantive progress was made on reconstruction.[3]

Arkansas seemed to be one Confederate state where disparate Unionist elements might coalesce into a unified movement. The state hosted a significant nonslaveholding population, and secession had provoked considerable opposition, though Unionists could do little during the war. By September 1863, federal forces under General Frederick Steele gained control of Little Rock and, at least nominally, most of the state. Steele employed a lenient policy toward white civilians, especially the planters, hoping to promote Unionism. In January 1864,

Unionist delegates representing fewer than half of the state's counties met in convention and wrote a constitution abolishing slavery and even allowing for black education and the apprenticeship system Lincoln had recommended. After miscommunication between Washington and Little Rock, an election was set for mid-March to ratify the constitution and elect a state government and congressmen. Lincoln named Steele "master," as he had with Nathaniel Banks in Louisiana, and encouraged Arkansas Unionists to work together. The campaign, however, amounted to the candidates questioning each other's past loyalties. Despite Confederate attempts to disrupt the election, voters overwhelmingly approved the constitution, making Arkansas the second Confederate state to abolish slavery. They also elected a state government and congressmen, and the new government was inaugurated. In May the legislature chose US senators.

From here, though, matters soured. Many protested the senatorial election of William M. Fishback, alleging his dubious loyalty during the secession crisis. Meanwhile, Steele's attempt to assist Banks's ill-fated Red River campaign in Louisiana had itself been a fiasco, helping to revive guerilla activity and destabilize federal control of the state. Senate debate over seating the members-elect focused on Fishback's loyalty and questioned the legitimacy of the whole Arkansas enterprise. With the war again going badly for the Union by late spring and early summer, and with congressional debate over the Wade-Davis bill inseparable from Arkansas (and Louisiana) affairs, the Senate voted overwhelmingly not to seat the claimants. Despite this defeat, Lincoln supported his Arkansas government, but nothing could be done to restore the state before the presidential election.[4]

These developments paled next to those in Louisiana, which had been a complex web even before Lincoln made Banks master. Lincoln had devised the ten-percent plan in large part to bring order to the situation there, but the results of the Louisiana experiment would be uncertain at best, notwithstanding the attention he devoted to it for the rest of his presidency.[5]

Banks moved quickly in early 1864 to carry out Lincoln's charge and to fulfill his own pledge of a timely restoration. He proposed a two-step process that included electing a new state government *before* writing a constitution abolishing slavery. Since this meant holding an election under the antebellum constitution, Banks suspended the constitution's slavery provisions. This plan ran counter to that of the radical wing of the Free State organization, headed by Thomas J. Durant, which wanted to write a new constitution abolishing slavery—and possibly adopting black suffrage while imposing political proscriptions on former Confederates—before electing a state government. Thus, Unionists divided over whether first to elect a new government or write a new constitution, with either course having important implications. Moreover, the radical faction had been responsible for the registry of voters, preparatory to a convention, that was to have taken place the previous year. In fact, it was the lack of progress over this registry that sparked Lincoln's November outburst and resulted in his placing Banks in charge. Thus, the radicals considered Banks's having been made "master," along with his decision to elect a state government before crafting a free-state constitution, as a repudiation of their vision for reconstructing Louisiana. The situation was exacerbated by Lincoln's approval of Banks's course, and by Banks's characteristically unwise remarks that cast doubt on the independence of a government created under his authority.

Banks scheduled an election for governor and other state officials for February 22 and another in April for delegates to a constitutional convention. The nominating process and campaigns formalized the moderate-radical split in the Free State organization. The moderates nominated Michael Hahn and the radicals Benjamin F. Flanders for governor. Both men had served briefly in Congress after winning elections in late 1862. Despite pledging neutrality, Banks clearly supported Hahn, and the army greatly assisted his campaign. The differences between the two candidates were arguably more apparent than real. Both supported emancipation, and while Hahn disavowed racial equality and employed overtly racialist rhetoric in his campaign, Flanders and the radicals at this point did not unequivocally endorse black suffrage.

Presidential politics also affected the contest. Several radical leaders held posts in the US Custom House in New Orleans. They supported treasury secretary Salmon P. Chase for the Republican presidential nomination and looked to him for assistance. The Banks-Hahn faction presented itself as the legitimate creation of the ten-percent plan and appealed to Lincoln. But because Louisiana had come to be seen as part of the presidential contest, and of the divide between Lincoln and the Radical Republicans, both men were wary of interfering. Lincoln, as usual, urged both groups to work together, but he was seen as favoring the Banks-Hahn faction.

Turnout for the February elections, which took place before those in Arkansas or Tennessee, amounted to one-fourth of the state-wide antebellum vote, though it approximated prewar levels for the occupied areas. Hahn was easily elected governor, and he and Banks pronounced the election an unqualified success, a vindication of Lincoln's plan, and a model for other states. Durant's radical faction denounced the whole process, and when its protest to Lincoln proved unavailing, it appealed to Congress to reject Lincoln's Louisiana government. Durant worked closely with congressional Republicans over the next year to achieve this goal, and Congress would ultimately reject the government. But with Ulysses S. Grant's promotion to command of the Union armies imminent, and amidst great hopes for the spring campaign, congressional Republicans were loath to challenge Lincoln. In early March, Hahn was inaugurated governor, and he and Banks prepared for the election of delegates to the constitutional convention. Banks also readied his military campaign to bring Louisiana's Red River region under Union control.

In mid-March, Lincoln penned one of his most frequently debated documents. In a letter marked *"Private,"* he congratulated Michael Hahn for "having fixed your name in history as the first-free-state Governor of Louisiana." Though technically incorrect, this description was presumably about to come true with the impending constitutional convention. With the convention also expected to consider the question of voting rights, Lincoln remarked: "I barely suggest for your private consideration, whether some of the colored people may not be let in—as, for instance, the very intelligent, and especially those who have fought gallantly in our ranks." This course, Lincoln further noted, "would probably help, in some trying time to come, to keep the jewel of liberty within the family of freedom," and he concluded this remarkable letter by specifying that "this is only a suggestion, not to the public, but to you alone."[6]

Whatever racial assumptions were embedded in his language or in how he framed the issue, Lincoln by early 1864 embraced black suffrage in principle. This was well before, as LaWanda Cox has demonstrated, Radical Republicans had generally done so. Lincoln had clearly given this matter considerable thought, but he was also probably coaxed toward this position in a White House meeting he held earlier that month with two prominent New Orleans free men of color, who, on behalf of that city's free black community, petitioned him for voting rights. Lincoln was sympathetic to the petitioners, but he responded to them the same way he had justified his emancipation policy: his main consideration was preserving the Union, and any attempt to impose black suffrage on a state would hinder that goal more than help it. Black suffrage might theoretically become a necessary war measure and a condition of a state's readmission, he reasoned, as had been the case with emancipation. However, such an eventuality was unlikely. Thus Lincoln probably believed that privately recommending limited black suffrage was as far as he could go.

The election for convention delegates, moved up to late March, was an overwhelming victory for the Hahn faction, since the radicals boycotted it, but turnout was much lower than that of the election for the state government. The convention gave Louisiana its 1864 constitution that formally abolished slavery, but it rejected even limited black suffrage. The convention at first dismissed black voting rights altogether, and only after Hahn made Lincoln's letter known did it authorize the state legislature to enact limited black suffrage, which was unlikely to happen. Although the constitution allowed for black education, it included no other provisions for securing black civil rights or equality before the law. Neither did it impose political proscriptions on former Confederates beyond Lincoln's future-loyalty oath. Notwithstanding its accomplishments, the convention had something of a farcical quality. It also had the misfortune to meet during Banks's disastrous Red River campaign of the spring, which, instead of gaining more Confederate territory, wound up undermining the entire free-state initiative. As in Arkansas, the constitution was slated for a popular vote, in early September.

Worse still, by the time the convention adjourned in July, the military and political situations had deteriorated dramatically. In addition to the Red River fiasco, Grant had suffered unspeakable losses in Virginia, Sherman seemed to be going nowhere in Georgia, and Confederate general Jubal Early had threatened Washington, DC, in early July. Lincoln gained the Republican presidential nomination in June, but he still faced the challenge of General John C. Frémont, whom a breakaway radical convention had nominated in late May. The Union war effort was floundering, and not only had the restoration of several seceded states under the ten-percent plan stalled after months of work, but Lincoln also faced a direct congressional challenge on the entire matter of reconstruction.

II

This challenge manifested itself during July and August 1864 in the dispute over the Wade-Davis bill. The work of Radical Republican leaders Benjamin F. Wade of Ohio in the Senate and Henry Winter Davis of Maryland in the House, the bill is generally considered the congressional—and Radical—alternative to Lincoln's ten-percent plan. Lincoln pocket-vetoed the measure by not signing it after Congress had adjourned, but he then took the unusual step of issuing a veto message, prompting a response from the bill's authors so scathing that it backfired and gained Lincoln further support. The dispute had several meanings: it represented genuine differences between Lincoln and congressional Republicans in general, not just the Radicals, over both reconstruction and the conduct of the war, at a time when the war was going badly for the Union; it constituted a legislative challenge to executive authority over reconstruction, especially when this authority was being used to establish governments of dubious "republican" character in the South; and it was part of the effort to replace Lincoln as the Republican (or "Union") presidential nominee, when his reelection prospects appeared decidedly dim. All these factors contributed to the controversy.[7]

The Wade-Davis bill resulted less from longstanding tensions between Lincoln and congressional Republicans over reconstruction than from growing dissatisfaction in early 1864 over events in the South, especially in Louisiana. Although Congress had considered reconstruction legislation designed to supplement Lincoln's plan, many Republicans became increasingly dismayed by the military's role in establishing the Louisiana government, civil rights, and Banks's labor policy. Lincoln had drafted the ten-percent plan with Louisiana in mind, and the Wade-Davis bill was likewise conceived in response to developments there. Inseparable from these considerations were the attempt to strike Lincoln from the Republican ticket and the failure of the House of Representatives to pass the constitutional amendment abolishing slavery after the Senate had done so in April. This setback left Wade-Davis as the sole measure on reconstruction before Congress at the end of its session. Although most Republican lawmakers had become convinced of the need for reconstruction legislation, the Wade-Davis bill passed only after complicated legislative maneuvering and intense debate during the session's final days. Some Republicans thought it had been pushed through too quickly.

In its final form, the bill—passage of which was partly overshadowed by Chase's resignation as treasury secretary and by Jubal Early's raid on Washington—differed significantly from Lincoln's ten-percent plan. Only after Confederate military defeat, per Wade-Davis, would the president appoint provisional governors to assume responsibility for restoring the seceded states. Once a majority of a state's white male population swore to uphold the US constitution, the provisional governor would authorize holding a state constitutional convention. Participation in the process of framing new constitutions—including electing delegates to the convention and serving at it—was restricted to white males who could take the "ironclad oath," swearing they had never aided the Confederacy. The bill required the new constitutions to abolish slavery, and it ensured the former slaves' freedom and effectively adopted Attorney General Edward Bates's 1862 decision that free black people were American citizens. It also included guarantees for equality before the law in certain instances, including trials, but it did not mandate black suffrage. The constitutions would have to be approved by a majority of a state's eligible white male voters, and by Congress, after which the state would rejoin the Union. Thus, the Wade-Davis bill postponed the question of reconstruction until the end of hostilities; it distinguished between white southerners who swore future loyalty and those who had never been disloyal; it required a majority of the white male population to swear loyalty before commencing reconstruction and restricted participation to those who could take the ironclad oath; it mandated framing new constitutions abolishing slavery before electing state governments or members to Congress; and it nudged the Republican Party and the nation toward racial equality.

Despite these differences, the ten-percent plan and the Wade-Davis bill also exhibited important similarities. Both plans called for abolishing slavery as a condition for restoring the seceded states to the Union (though Lincoln's did so implicitly), but without mandating black suffrage. Wade-Davis also resembled the ten-percent plan by excluding provisions concerning land confiscation or other economic matters, recognizing a presidential role in reconstruction, and stopping short of full-fledged equality before the law. Moreover, the Wade-Davis bill rejected territorialization and other radical theories and instead invoked the constitutional principle of guaranteeing "republican" governments in the states—as did Lincoln's plan. While both plans greatly expanded federal power within the states, if to varying degrees, they did so from an essentially conservative position. Congressional debate over the Wade-Davis bill focused more on the Louisiana and Arkansas governments than on the ten-percent plan, and, as Herman Belz has argued, it reflected moderate rather than radical thinking and marked a compromise among congressional Republicans.

Nonetheless, the episode reflected important philosophical differences over the war and reconstruction and over the link between military and political goals. By postponing reconstruction until hostilities ended, the Wade-Davis bill separated the war from postwar reconstruction, whereas Lincoln's plan, especially insofar as it reflected his restorationist thinking, envisioned the war as part of the process of restoring federal authority over the seceded states.

Lincoln offered amnesty, and the opportunity to participate in the restoration process, in return for pledging future loyalty and abiding by emancipation, while Wade-Davis, by restricting participation to genuine Unionists, sought to replace the South's traditional leadership. Although Lincoln excluded high-ranking Confederates from his amnesty, he allowed for their possible future inclusion. Wade-Davis envisioned no such future leniency. On the question of race, Wade-Davis did not require black suffrage, but it would have made citizens of the former slaves and employed federal power to begin implementing racial equality. And some of its supporters envisaged black suffrage in the foreseeable future. Lincoln included no such provision, even though he was reconceptualizing black freedom. Thus, while the ten-percent plan in certain respects reflected the more limited, restorationist dimension of Lincoln's approach to reconstruction, Wade-Davis envisioned the larger reconstruction of southern society, which could not commence until the rebellion had been suppressed.

It was perhaps in their broader conceptualizations of the rebellion, and in what its suppression meant for the postwar settlement, where the two plans differed most. Although Lincoln had long since realized that the Confederacy enjoyed mass popular support, he also believed its adherents could be induced to renounce their Confederate loyalty and resume their allegiance to the Union. For Lincoln this is what the war was essentially about. Since the war and reconstruction were inseparable, it was entirely logical that Lincoln would put forward a "wartime" reconstruction plan. Emancipation may have irrevocably transformed the war, but Lincoln was still pursuing a policy of conciliation. The ten-percent plan's amnesty provision, which underlay Lincoln's entire approach to reconstruction, would serve a function akin to the principle of Christian reconciliation: past acts were to be forgiven in return for a vow to sin no more. "On principle I dislike an oath which requires a man to swear he *has* not done wrong," Lincoln had previously observed. "It rejects the Christian principle of forgiveness on terms of repentance. I think it is enough if the man does no wrong *hereafter*." For Lincoln, Confederates could be persuaded to return to the Union, though they must accept emancipation, and he offered them as an incentive the opportunity to participate in shaping the postwar settlement. Although this sentiment was genuine, by mid-1864 Lincoln's increasing solicitude for black freedom was already bringing him to a serious reconsideration of this position.[8]

The Wade-Davis bill drew on diametrically opposing assumptions. In essence, it rejected conciliation and presupposed a war of conquest. The political revolution that the bill envisioned could not be accomplished in the midst of war but would have to await Confederate defeat. Recognizing that the Confederacy enjoyed broad support, and yet also concerned with American traditions of majority rule and consent of the governed, it required a majority to affirm its loyalty before starting reconstruction. It offered no inducements to Confederates, instead presuming them to be irredeemably disloyal and prohibiting them from the process of reconstruction. They might later be politically rehabilitated, but not until reconstruction was completed. For Congress, only Unionists whose loyalties were beyond question could be entrusted with the power and responsibility of framing new state constitutions and governments. Although the Wade-Davis bill did not explicitly mandate the wholesale restructuring of southern society, it saw recasting the South's political landscape as an essential first step.

Lincoln expressed no opinion on the bill and exerted no influence on congressional deliberations, and Congress expected him to approve it. Because Congress passed the bill within the session's last ten days, Lincoln could veto it by taking no action. And that is exactly what he did, catching Congress very much by surprise. On July 8, Lincoln explained his decision in a highly unusual proclamation, in which he overlooked theory and focused mostly on practical considerations. Employing conciliatory language, he refrained from becoming "inflexibly committed to any single plan of restoration." Neither would he declare, by approving the bill, "that the free-state constitutions and governments, already adopted and installed in Arkansas and Louisiana, shall be set aside and held for nought, thereby repelling and discouraging the loyal citizens who have set up the same, as to further effort." As he had previously done many times, he denied congressional authority to abolish slavery in the states, while explicitly endorsing the constitutional amendment abolishing slavery. At the same time, Lincoln approved of the measure in principle, declaring himself "fully satisfied with the system for restoration contained in the bill, as one very proper plan for the loyal people of any State choosing to adopt it." However disingenuous this disclaimer might seem, since Confederates were unlikely to countenance the Wade-Davis plan, southern Unionists who could meet the ironclad oath might prefer it. Lincoln therefore pledged to provide all necessary assistance, including appointing military governors (though the bill specified provisional governors), to the loyal people of any state once the rebellion had been suppressed within it and its people had resumed their allegiance to the Union. In short, Lincoln assented to Congress's plan in theory though not in practice, since it would compel him to repudiate work already completed toward reconstruction and demoralize those who had undertaken it. But were southern Unionists to initiate reconstruction under Wade-Davis, he would comply with its provisions.[9]

The proclamation largely achieved its desired effect. The public perceived no irreparable split between Lincoln and Congress, and some Republicans admitted to having handled the matter poorly and regretted the bill's passage. Despite Lincoln's attempt to navigate intraparty and executive-legislative differences, his action provoked angry recriminations. The Radicals' resentment may have festered less over reconstruction than over the administration's conduct of the war, but the veto served as a lightning rod. On August 5, Wade and Davis issued their "manifesto," accusing Lincoln of, among other transgressions, "dictatorial usurpation." Lincoln ignored the will of Congress, they charged, especially in defending "those shadows of Governments" in Arkansas and Louisiana, which "are the mere creatures of his will." Those governments were "mere oligarchies," they continued, "imposed on the people by military orders under the forms of election, at which generals, provost-marshals, soldiers and camp-followers were the chief actors, assisted by a handful of resident citizens, and urged on to premature action by private letters from the President." Lincoln was trying to manipulate the presidential election by controlling the reconstructed states' electoral votes, which he held "at the dictation of his personal ambition." They took special umbrage at Lincoln's intention to implement the bill, if called on to do so, without authority of law. Lincoln had to recognize that "the authority of Congress is paramount and must be respected," and they recommended he confine himself to enforcing rather than making the law, "and leave political reorganization to Congress."[10]

The manifesto created an initial stir, but it proved short-lived. It was so intemperate that it actually worked to Lincoln's benefit. Although the effort to replace Lincoln continued, almost all Republicans eventually recognized the need for party unity, especially after the Democratic national convention in late August, and both Wade and Davis ultimately endorsed Lincoln for reelection. Though hardly inconsequential, the Wade-Davis controversy would not derail the party from achieving the goals of carrying the election, winning the war, and securing emancipation, which were coming to be seen as inseparable. The dispute revealed the potential for divisions between Lincoln and congressional Republicans, especially the Radicals, over postwar policy, assuming one would be needed, but it did not foreshadow an inevitable intraparty schism had Lincoln not been assassinated. The Wade-Davis episode was not even the most serious political crisis Lincoln faced that summer, as he confronted renewed calls to negotiate with the Confederacy and retract the Emancipation Proclamation.

III

Lincoln had designed the ten-percent plan, in part, to prevent a restoration of the seceded states to the Union with slavery intact, but uneven progress under the plan by mid-1864 increased the prospects of that very outcome. The military situation by summer may have obviated talk of reconstruction. However, just as they had done before the Union victories at Gettysburg and Vicksburg, some of Lincoln's northern critics used military failure to bolster their calls for negotiating with the Confederacy and retracting the Emancipation Proclamation. Thus, the ten-percent plan did not eliminate for Lincoln the danger of a Confederate offer of peace and reunion in exchange for slavery. Throughout winter and spring 1864, Lincoln continued to argue that abolishing slavery was essential and not incidental to preserving—actually reconstructing—the Union. By summer, these issues were intertwined with the presidential election. Even as Lincoln confronted fallout from the Wade-Davis dispute and radical efforts to replace him as the Republican nominee, he likewise faced renewed calls for negotiations and charges that his emancipation policy was preventing peace.

No sooner had Lincoln issued the Wade-Davis veto proclamation than he wrestled with another awkward attempt at diplomacy by Horace Greeley, the mercurial newspaper editor. Greeley informed Lincoln in early July that representatives of the Confederate government on the Canadian side of Niagara Falls were authorized to negotiate. Lincoln was uninterested in Confederate peace terms, and he trusted neither Greeley nor the supposed emissaries, whom he correctly suspected of meddling in the presidential election. Yet Lincoln had to strike a balance between, on the one hand, adhering to military victory and maintaining support for the war, and, on the other, at least appearing open to Confederate overtures that might end the nation's suffering. He therefore called Greeley's bluff, authorizing Greeley himself to bring to Washington "any person anywhere professing to have any proposition of Jefferson Davis, in writing, for peace, embracing the restoration of the Union and abandonment of slavery." Despite Greeley's objection to the appointment, Lincoln insisted on it. He also sent his secretary John Hay to Niagara Falls with a letter specifying the terms under which Lincoln would meet with the Confederate officials.[11]

In the letter, addressed "To Whom it may concern," Lincoln avowed that "[a]ny proposition which embraces the restoration of peace, the integrity of the whole Union, and the abandonment of slavery . . . will be received and considered by the Executive government of the United States." Such a proposition "will be met by liberal terms on other substantial and collateral points." Lincoln was appearing to offer reasonable terms to the Confederates in exchange for entering into negotiations, which he had always opposed. Everything was up for discussion so long as the Confederate government agreed to restoration of the Union and the "abandonment" of slavery. Yet Lincoln obviously knew the Confederates could never accept these conditions. Lincoln's stance on the Union was familiar enough, but his demand that the Confederacy give up slavery went beyond any previous federal measures. Indeed, such a condition, in light of the recent failure of the constitutional amendment, must have struck the emissaries as audacious.[12]

Lincoln's strategy also involved risk. By presenting conditions tantamount to Confederate surrender, he was sabotaging the Greeley initiative, but he was also opening himself to charges from his northern opponents of jeopardizing the chances of peace and Union by demanding the end of slavery. Lincoln also knew that the Confederates would never consent to "the integrity of the whole Union," let alone to abandoning slavery. Yet because he could not run the risk of a peace overture that included Union but not emancipation, he had to stand firm on emancipation. The Confederates still might try to call his bluff, just as he had called Greeley's, if only to put him in a bind. Lincoln may be seen here as attempting to undermine negotiations under any circumstances, and thus motivated more by a desire to preserve the Union than to end slavery. But his focus on emancipation, especially so close to an election it appeared he might lose, showed his commitment to it.

Lincoln had made an important point, but when the Confederate emissaries had the letter published, it caused much consternation among War Democrats and even some conservative Republicans. In mid-August, for example, Lincoln received a letter from Charles D. Robinson, a Democratic Wisconsin newspaper editor, underscoring this discontent. Robinson explained that he and other War Democrats had hitherto supported Lincoln's war policy, including military emancipation, as a necessary means to suppressing the rebellion. However, "your declaration . . . that no steps can be taken towards peace . . . unless accompanied with an abandonment of slavery," Robinson argued, "puts the whole war question on a new basis, and takes us War Democrats clear off our feet, leaving us no ground to stand upon." Robinson wrote, he assured Lincoln, not to find fault with Lincoln's policy, "but in the hope that you may suggest some interpretation of it, as will . . . make it tenable ground on which we War Democrats may stand."

Robinson's letter was not the usual partisan vitriol but a sober critique that Lincoln could not ignore, and he immediately drafted a response. The openness of the "To Whom" letter, however, and the cogency of Robinson's argument, forced Lincoln into logical contortions and evasions. "To me it seems plain that saying re-union and abandonment of slavery would be considered, if offered," Lincoln began, "is not saying that nothing *else* or *less* would be considered, if offered." But this is precisely what he had said. Lincoln was skirting the issue that the "To Whom" letter—far from merely indicating his willingness to consider a Confederate peace offer based on reunion and abandoning slavery, or from even hinting he might consider anything less—had virtually demanded that any Confederate peace offer include both reunion and the abolition of slavery. In effect, by specifying he would consider any proposition that included these two preconditions, Lincoln implied he would never consider any proposal that did not include both of them. Perhaps recognizing his own sophistry, Lincoln added: "But I will not stand upon the mere construction of language." His letter went on to defend emancipation and black enlistment on the pragmatic grounds that, were the proclamation to be rescinded, black people would withdraw their support for the Union and the war effort would go down to defeat. However, this time Lincoln expressed this idea in especially concrete terms, employing a formulation he would use again in the future. "It is not a question of sentiment or taste," he insisted, in describing the black contribution to the war, "but one of physical force, which may be measured, and estimated as horsepower, and steam power, are measured and estimated. And by measurement, it is more than we can lose, and live." Still, Lincoln sidestepped Robinson's charge that the "To Whom" letter, by going beyond the Emancipation Proclamation, had placed "the whole war question on a new basis." Neither did it offer Robinson a way for Democrats to support an abolitionist war.

If Lincoln's letter provided War Democrats little solace, its conclusion might have alarmed Radicals. "Allow me to remind you," Lincoln began the last paragraph, redirecting Robinson's attention to the larger context, "that no one, having control of the rebel armies, or, in fact, having any influence whatever in the rebellion, has offered, or intimated a willingness to, a restoration of the Union, in any event or on any condition whatever. Let it be constantly borne in mind that no such offer has been made or intimated." The main obstacle to peace, Lincoln also reminded Robinson, was neither military emancipation nor the proposed constitutional amendment abolishing slavery, but rather the seceded states' forcible attempt at independence. Why should Unionists bicker, Lincoln asked, over "an abstract question" that the enemy "refuses to present as a practical one?" Lincoln's language to this point might have heartened Radicals, but his final sentence would not have. "If Jefferson Davis wishes, for himself, or for the benefit of his friends at the North, to know what I would do if he were to offer peace and re-union, saying nothing about slavery," Lincoln suggested, "let him try me."[13]

Lincoln anticipated the outcry that even a hint of backtracking on emancipation would provoke. He therefore discussed the Robinson letter, as he often did in such situations, with several White House visitors before deciding whether to send it. In a meeting with former Wisconsin governor Alexander W. Randall and Wisconsin judge Joseph T. Mills, a synopsis of which was later published in newspapers, Lincoln revealed his inclinations by defending emancipation on both practical and idealistic grounds. Should the Democrats win the election, he argued, they would conduct a war of "conciliation" and rescind emancipation, resulting in a loss of black support the Union could ill afford: "we would be compelled to abandon the war in 3 weeks." Moreover, were he to rescind emancipation, he would "be damned in time & in eternity for so doing"; instead, "the world shall know that I will keep my faith to friends & enemies, come what will." To the charge of his prosecuting an abolitionist war, he responded: "It is & will be carried on so long as I am President for the sole purpose of restoring the Union. But no human power can subdue this rebellion without using the Emancipation lever as I have done." Lincoln may have been trying to persuade himself to shelve the Robinson letter, but a meeting later that day with the black abolitionist Frederick Douglass settled the issue. After they had discussed the situation at length, as Douglass later wrote, Lincoln asked him: "Shall I send forth this letter[?]" Douglass answered: "Certainly not.

It would be given a broader meaning than you intend to convey; it would be taken as a complete surrender of your anti-slavery policy, and do you serious damage." Lincoln took what amounted to his own advice and did not reply to Robinson.[14]

Lincoln may have abandoned trying to mollify War Democrats in this instance (though they remained integral to the war coalition), but he still faced criticism from moderate and conservative Republicans similarly disturbed by his evident demand for the abolition of slavery. Such criticism missed Lincoln's point of slavery's effective irrelevance, since Confederates would accept nothing less than independence. It also overlooked his point that, because the Confederacy was illegitimate, negotiations on any terms were out of the question. Yet the fact that so many northerners attributed the interminable bloodletting to Lincoln's emancipation policy rather than to the rebellion itself posed a seemingly intractable problem.

Henry J. Raymond pinpointed this difficulty and suggested a solution. As editor of the *New York Times* and chairman of the National Union Executive Committee, Raymond reflected centrist Republican opinion. On August 22, he penned what must have been a dispiriting letter for Lincoln to read. Observing that "the tide is setting strongly against us," Raymond identified as a key cause the general impression "that we are not to have peace *in any event* under this administration until Slavery is abandoned." Somehow, the idea that "we *can* have peace with Union if we would" had gained hold of the public mind. It was useless to reason with or denounce this belief, Raymond argued; instead, it must be refuted by some bold and authoritative act. Therefore, he suggested that Lincoln appoint a commission to offer peace to Jefferson Davis, "*on the sole condition of acknowledging the supremacy of the constitution*," with all other questions to be settled by a national convention. Davis was sure to reject this offer, Raymond believed, and his action would "dispel all the delusions about peace that prevail in the North." It would undermine Democratic opposition to the administration, galvanize public support for the war, and "unite the North as nothing since [the] firing on Fort Sumter has hitherto done." Lincoln undoubtedly recognized in Raymond's proposal his own logic in the Robinson letter, since Raymond was less intent on rescinding emancipation than on proving that the Confederate leadership opposed any peace short of independence, irrespective of slavery.

It is indicative of Lincoln's desperation that on August 23, having received Raymond's letter, he wrote and had the cabinet blindly endorse his famous memorandum, acknowledging his probable re-election failure and pledging to cooperate with the president-elect to save the Union before the inauguration, "as he will have secured his election on such ground that he can not possibly save it afterwards." Lincoln was no doubt convinced that a Democratic victory in the election would mean a cessation of hostilities and an end to the war. Yet even insofar as the War Democrats pledged to fight a war for Union and not for emancipation, Lincoln believed that such a strategy was equally doomed. Thus, emancipation—which for Republicans now meant the abolition of slavery—was essential to Union victory. Nonetheless, the next day Lincoln drafted a response to Raymond's proposal, appointing Raymond himself as emissary to Jefferson Davis and instructing him to propose "that upon the restoration of the Union and the national authority, the war shall cease at once, all remaining questions to be left for adjustment by peaceful means." Were Davis to reject this offer, Raymond was to enquire whether there were any terms he would accept. Having drafted the proposal, Lincoln discussed it in an August 25 meeting with Raymond and several cabinet members, and, according to Lincoln's secretary John G. Nicolay, Raymond "very readily concurred with them in the opinion that to follow his plan of sending a commission to Richmond would be worse than losing the Presidential contest—it would be ignominiously surrendering it in advance." Although Raymond's proposal contained an indisputable logic, as did Lincoln's own "try me" suggestion, Lincoln clearly saw, as Frederick Douglass had expressed it, that public opinion would deem the initiative a "complete surrender" of his emancipation policy, and he scrapped the plan.[15]

Lincoln had decided against entertaining a Confederate peace offer that required modification of his emancipation policy, but he could not overlook public misperception of it. Thus, in mid-September he drafted a letter, to be read at a mass rally in Buffalo, in which he again showed the inseparability of negotiations, emancipation, and black support for the war. "Much is being said about peace," Lincoln began, and while no one wanted peace more than he did, he was "yet unprepared to give up the Union for a peace which, so achieved, could not be of much duration." The war had been commenced to destroy the Union, he reminded his audience, and so he accepted it as necessary and was conducting it solely to save the Union. "An armistice—a cessation of hostilities—is the end of the struggle, and the insurgents would be in peaceable possession of all that has been struggled for." Not only must negotiations be rejected, but emancipation defended. "Any different policy in regard to the colored man, deprives us of his help, and this is more than we can bear." The Union war effort simply could not continue without black support. "This is not a question of sentiment or taste," he insisted, again using language from the Robinson letter, "but one of physical force which may be measured and estimated as horse-power and Steam-power are measured and estimated. Keep it and you can save the Union. Throw it away, and the Union goes with it." Neither could the Union retain black people's support "with the express or implied understanding that upon the first convenient occasion, they are to be re-inslaved." "It *can* not be," he concluded, "and it *ought* not to be." As with the Robinson letter, Lincoln never sent this one, though more because of practical difficulties than doubts about its content. And while the Union's improved military fortunes by mid-September undermined calls for negotiations, Lincoln had reaffirmed his commitment, after perhaps a momentary lapse, to "the abandonment of slavery" as the principle on which the Union would be reconstructed.[16]

IV

When Lincoln met with Frederick Douglass in late August, the main topic of discussion was not the Robinson letter but another problem Lincoln was contemplating. Convinced he would lose the election and the new Democratic president would stop the war, leaving the large majority of the Confederacy's slaves in bondage, Lincoln expressed disappointment that more slaves had not reached Union lines and gained freedom under the Emancipation Proclamation. Douglass believed this problem stemmed from the slaveholders' ability to stifle news of the proclamation, and so Lincoln proposed that Douglass devise some means of informing the slaves and bringing them into Union territory. After further discussion, Douglass agreed to organize a group of black scouts, who, with federal military assistance, would spread word of the proclamation in the Confederate interior and help free as many slaves as possible before Lincoln left office and the war was halted.

Lincoln's proposal was audacious, not to say fantastical, and Douglass could not help but be struck by it. The two men had met once before, a year earlier, and although Douglass's criticism of Lincoln had softened since the proclamation, he had remained among the most consistent of Lincoln's radical detractors. Now, Douglass was genuinely moved by Lincoln's commitment to black freedom, especially given the pressure Lincoln was under from his own allies. As James Oakes has observed, that meeting "changed forever" how Douglass viewed Lincoln. He now saw in Lincoln, as Douglass later wrote, "a deeper moral conviction against slavery than I had ever seen before in anything spoken or written by him."[17]

While the transformation of Douglass's opinion of Lincoln was profound, it was also indicative of Lincoln's own evolution on black freedom. By mid-1864, Lincoln had essentially repudiated positions he had held only two years earlier. The former Lincoln—who had advocated gradual, compensated emancipation, to be undertaken with the slaveholders' consent; who had endorsed colonization in principle, and who as president had explored several colonization schemes, even sponsoring one that failed spectacularly; who had reflected the racism pervasive of his time and had pandered to it for political gain; and who could not envision black people as essential to American society—was now hardly recognizable. In addition to issuing the Emancipation Proclamation, Lincoln had approved every congressional wartime measure undermining slavery or advancing black freedom. He had let stand the attorney general's ruling that free black people were American citizens. And although Lincoln had remained noncommittal during congressional debate on the Thirteenth Amendment, he now endorsed it and called for its inclusion in the Republican platform for the presidential election. He likewise contributed to the emerging Republican consensus on the principle of equality before the law, and he had endorsed (though privately) limited black suffrage. In a broader sense, Lincoln had significantly reconceptualized black freedom and its implications for American democracy, citizenship, and liberty. These concepts, so central to American life, would assume a transcendent, universal quality, as the nation would finally realize its own ideals.

Essential to Lincoln's redefining of black freedom was the contribution of black troops to the Union war effort. The historic link between citizenship and military service has often been noted, and Lincoln was no less influenced by it. Lincoln defended emancipation on idealistic grounds as well as on the pragmatic, almost concrete, grounds that black support, especially black military service, was essential to Union success. Lincoln perhaps assumed that black people would support only a Union that did not include slavery, but he also came to believe that the new nation was indebted to the black Americans who were helping to make it. So long as Lincoln's reelection remained uncertain, Union military victory and securing emancipation took precedence over racial equality. Moreover, even by his death Lincoln had not quite fully embraced equality before the law or black suffrage. Nonetheless, given whence Lincoln had started and the trajectory of his racial thought, the inexorable logic of American freedom now that slavery was to be abolished, and the circumstances in a postwar South that Lincoln would have confronted, his eventual support for black legal and political equality is hardly implausible.

There is no doubt, as Eric Foner has observed, that Lincoln experienced something of a spiritual transformation during the war— brought on by the 1862 death of his beloved son Willie; by the deaths of personal friends, political associates, and his wife's family members in the war; and by the deaths of hundreds of thousands of (to him) nameless Americans, as a result of his election to the presidency and determination to prosecute a war of unconditional surrender. Lincoln had always demonstrated a capacity for personal growth, and he had already moved significantly on slavery, though less on racial equality, before the war. Since becoming president, he had been exposed to a wider variety of opinion and had come into personal contact with many more accomplished, successful black people than he had in Illinois. Lincoln also displayed throughout his life, especially after what Michael Burlingame has called his mid-life crisis of 1849–1854, a fundamental humility, an awareness of his own imperfections and fallibility, an ability to consider alternative viewpoints and to see the world through the eyes of others. If Frederick Douglass—who, as James Oakes has shown, experienced his own wartime transformation—was moved to change his opinion of Abraham Lincoln after that August 1864 meeting, it was because he was dealing with a very different Lincoln.[18]

Yet there was one aspect of reconstruction where Lincoln's previous experiences and overall outlook might have become a handicap rather than an advantage: the social and economic reconstruction of southern society. Lincoln's main critique of slavery had been that it robbed the slaves of the fruits of their labor—a point that assumed greater salience when juxtaposed to the virtues of northern free-labor society. The North may not have gone to war initially to remake the South, but such is what the war had become. Almost from the start, as federal forces gained Confederate territory, and as fugitive slaves took flight from the plantations, Union military and civilian authorities, along with northern reformers, initiated various free-labor arrangements in the South. Along the Atlantic seaboard, across the upper South, and throughout the Mississippi Valley, free-labor experiments had yielded mixed success. These programs were improvised solutions to the immediate problem of dislocation rather than carefully crafted blueprints for a postemancipation South. Still, reformers envisioned them as training grounds for instilling in former slaves the habits and ideas necessary to compete within a capitalist economy. Lincoln at first took only mild interest in wartime free labor, but following the Emancipation Proclamation, this interest grew. By 1864, he had become very much aware of the plight of formerly enslaved workers on southern plantations, especially in Louisiana, where military labor policy intersected with debate over that state's Unionist government.

Once Lincoln finally abandoned the colonization fantasy and began to think seriously about the consequences of emancipation for the South's labor system, he initially expressed support for some version of apprenticeship, usually linked to gradual abolition and an educational program to prepare former slaves for the challenges of freedom. During the nineteenth century, especially in debates over postemancipation labor, "apprenticeship" was often understood, by both supporters and detractors, as code for keeping former slaves bound to the plantations, even though the worst features of slavery were eliminated. Most of the northern states had adopted some version of apprenticeship when they had abolished slavery during the late eighteenth and early nineteenth centuries. During the 1830s, the British had attempted to replace Caribbean slavery with a form of apprenticeship that almost immediately collapsed because of the former slaves' opposition. Although Lincoln offered Confederates a voice in determining the new labor system as an inducement to resume their former loyalty, he genuinely seemed to have thought of apprenticeship as a temporary condition, one in which former slaves, as the ten-percent plan specified, would be protected from "abuse." Even to the degree Lincoln believed former slaves would require some form of preparation for life after emancipation, he likely did so—as did many nineteenth-century reformers—not because he deemed black people incapable of undertaking voluntary labor but because slavery had not provided them an environment conducive to internalizing the habits and values essential to success in the competitive marketplace. Once the conditions under which they worked had been changed and the interim training period completed, former slaves would be ready (presumably, since this idea for Lincoln was more implied than explicitly stated) to function in free-labor society.

By 1864, as the Thirteenth Amendment (despite its House failure) and emancipation in several states rendered gradualism increasingly moot, and as the repressive character of wartime free labor became more widely known and subject to criticism, Lincoln seemed to express misgivings over apprenticeship and over former slaves occupying an interim status as quasi-free laborers. In correspondence and public remarks during that year, he was decidedly more solicitous than he had been previously of the conditions of former slaves on plantations in the occupied South. In an April speech before the Sanitary Fair in Baltimore, for example, he employed a metaphor on the contested definition of freedom that likened former slaves to sheep and southern slaveholders to wolves—with himself, perhaps representing the federal government, playing the role of shepherd, who "drives the wolf from the sheep's throat." For someone who chose his words as carefully as he did, and who had long condemned slavery but not the slaveholders, Lincoln was perhaps coming to see that the main challenge in remaking southern society would come not from the former slaves but the dispossessed slaveholders.[19]

As his comments suggest, Lincoln may have begun to think substantively about the transformation of the South's labor system and the remaking of southern society. Yet there is little evidence that Lincoln had begun, even by the end of his life, to conceptualize an approach to the intractable difficulties that would arise from attempting to recast the plantation South along the lines of the free-labor North. In theory, any attempt to apply the free-labor ideology to a plantation society would have been a daunting challenge, but the bitter legacy of racial slavery would render that task virtually impossible. Indeed, the nation's inability to address the social and economic inequalities that slavery created stands as one of the central factors in the failure of postwar reconstruction. Because Lincoln believed deeply in the virtues of northern free-labor society, he would have been ill-equipped to reconcile the contradictions that inevitably arose from the attempt to reconstruct the slave South in the image of the free-labor North. Lincoln's metaphor acknowledged the inescapable conflict between the wolves and sheep, the former slaveholders and former slaves, but it could not offer a means for resolving such conflict, since the free-labor vision, which assumed harmony between capital and labor, formed the basis of Lincoln's thought. Neither did Lincoln's longstanding belief in the superiority of labor over capital—rooted as it was in the northern world of small, independent property holders and producers—provide a viable model for the postemancipation South.

Lincoln had at least begun to contemplate the question of labor as an element of reconstruction, but the same could not be said about land, in particular black landholding. Wartime free labor in certain parts of the South had allowed former slaves considerable access to land, mostly on abandoned and confiscated plantations. Building on nineteenth-century American notions of propertied independence, as well as on communal conceptions of property grounded in the collective slave experience, former slaves saw land, and productive property in general, as essential to a meaningful freedom. Black landholding would have required a federal program of wholesale property confiscation and redistribution, which themselves would have signified a revolutionary transformation of the southern social order and an unprecedented expansion of the power of the federal government. Such governmental intervention in society and the economy remained beyond the ken of most Americans, and Lincoln himself gave the matter no serious thought. He saw neither the wartime confiscation acts nor the federal 1862 Direct Tax Act, which specifically allowed for land confiscation, as mechanisms for bringing revolutionary change to the South.

Lincoln's approach to property, as was the case with everything else during the war, was motivated by the goals of regaining the allegiance of white southerners and ending the rebellion. This is why the ten-percent plan's pardon restored all property rights, except slaves. Such a strategy was driven not merely by pragmatism, for Lincoln temperamentally opposed radical solutions, especially any violation of the sanctity of property. Slavery, in a sense, may have been exceptional. And yet, for all of his hatred of slavery, Lincoln acquiesced to the slaveholders' property rights, based on a system of common law to which he was devoted. It is thus all but impossible to envision him subscribing to the kinds of measures that would have been required to bring about the economic and political destruction of the southern planter elite. As a moderate, centrist Republican, Lincoln, had he lived, would have faced the challenge, as others of his ilk later did, of steering a course between southern white intransigence and the advocates of confiscation and other radical measures. Generations of Americans, obsessed with Lincoln and race, have pondered the implications for American history had Lincoln lived to oversee postwar reconstruction. But the limits of Lincoln's approach to reconstruction would have been reached not on matters relating to race and civil rights, strictly speaking, but rather on those relating to the social and economic reconstruction of southern society.

V

Just as the prospects for Lincoln's reelection seemed bleakest, they suddenly brightened. The Democratic convention met in Chicago in late August and nominated former Union commander George B. McClellan for president. Although a War Democrat, McClellan had been Lincoln's nemesis as military commander, and his nomination pushed wavering Republicans back to the party fold. The convention also passed a peace platform, including a plank labeling the war a "failure" that McClellan himself repudiated. By early September, Atlanta had surrendered, as had the last Confederate fort protecting Mobile Bay, leaving Wilmington, North Carolina, the last Confederate port. These developments did not guarantee Lincoln reelection, but they profoundly altered the war's complexion, even as Grant and Lee remained locked at Petersburg.

During the next two months, momentum swelled behind the Republican campaign and Union war effort. Radical opposition to Lincoln finally collapsed with John C. Frémont's withdrawal from the contest and the death of US Supreme Court Chief Justice Roger B. Taney, whose expected replacement was Salmon Chase. Republican victories in several northern state elections, though close, were good omens, and Nevada's admission to the Union assured Lincoln of its electoral votes. Union general Philip Sheridan cleared Confederate forces from the Shenandoah Valley in October, and arrangements were made for Union soldiers to be furloughed for the election or to vote in the field. Throughout the North, abolitionists, editors, preachers, and other shapers of public opinion endorsed Lincoln, who suddenly looked very appealing with McClellan and Peace Democrats as the alternative. Still, with a close election expected, Republicans were not taking victory for granted.

Developments in the southern states showed glimmers of hope but disappointment, too. In September, voters in Unionist Louisiana approved the free-state constitution, formally abolishing slavery, and in October, Maryland voters did the same. Four of fifteen states (these two, Virginia, and Arkansas) had now abolished slavery, but events elsewhere were less encouraging. A fledgling reconstruction effort in northern Alabama, prompted by the ten-percent plan, had made little headway during the first half of 1864, and Sherman's summer campaign in northwest Georgia further destabilized the area. By fall, a resolution was introduced in the state legislature that called for negotiations with the federal government—in the event of a Democratic victory in the election—to restore Alabama to the Union with slavery intact. The resolution was sold as a means of undermining Lincoln's electoral chances and the Union war effort, but it spawned widespread talk of Alabama leaving the Confederacy, and the legislature defeated it amidst accusations of treason. Following the fall of Atlanta, Sherman authorized Augustus R. Wright, a former US and Confederate congressman from northwest Georgia, to travel to Washington to confer with Lincoln on that state's restoration. Perhaps suspecting Wright's other motives—he also sought the return of cotton federal troops had seized—Lincoln provided him with no specific instructions concerning reconstruction. Sherman's capture of Savannah in December led to a small upsurge of popular sentiment for Georgia's restoration, but no Confederate official supported it. Despite Union military victories in the state, reconstruction in Georgia remained dormant.[20]

However disappointing these developments, Alabama and Georgia were of secondary political importance. Arkansas, Louisiana, and Tennessee, by contrast, were of much greater significance—which, paradoxically, made developments in them all the more discouraging. Despite Congress's refusal to seat the Arkansas claimants and thus recognize the Arkansas government, Lincoln at first pledged to support it. The government struggled to maintain its authority during summer and fall against Confederate raids and guerilla attacks, and when Arkansas governor Isaac Murphy petitioned Lincoln for more military support, Lincoln remained oddly unresponsive. Then, as criticism mounted on military grounds against General Frederick Steele, the commander at Little Rock whose reconstruction efforts won him Arkansas Unionists' support, Lincoln initially endorsed Steele. But when Steele's commander, General E. R. S.

Canby, removed him after the November election, Lincoln refused to intervene. Although Lincoln supported the Arkansas government till the end, he may have been genuinely sensitive to Democratic charges of his trying to ram the readmission of Arkansas, Louisiana, and Tennessee through Congress so as to control their electoral votes. And even though he may have despaired over the Murphy government's weakness, he was probably unwilling to countermand an order issued out of military necessity.[21]

In Louisiana, approval of the new constitution was one bright spot in a situation that otherwise continued to frustrate Lincoln. At the same time they approved the constitution, voters also chose a new state legislature and members to Congress in elections dominated by the moderate, Banks-Hahn faction of the Free State organization. Internecine strife continued between these moderates and the radical faction of Thomas J. Durant and Benjamin Flanders, which consisted largely of treasury department appointees at the New Orleans Custom House. Some radicals even worked to defeat the constitution. Governor Hahn implored Lincoln to purge the radicals, but with the election approaching, Lincoln declined. In October, the legislature elected two US senators, who left for Washington in expectation of being seated when Congress reconvened in December; it also took the unusual step of selecting presidential electors, even though no general election was to take place. (Congress ultimately did not count Louisiana's electoral votes.) At Hahn's urging, the legislature began the process of legally defining black freedom, but it made little progress before the presidential election.

Yet Lincoln's biggest headache in Louisiana, as was so often the case there and elsewhere, came from friction between military commanders and the civilian government. With Banks in Washington during the fall, lobbying former congressional colleagues to recognize the Louisiana government he had helped create, his replacement, General Stephen Hurlbut, formerly an Illinois political associate of Lincoln, continually meddled in civilian affairs. Indeed, both Hurlbut and his superior, Canby, expressed open contempt in their official correspondence for Hahn's government, contending that until Louisiana was represented in Congress, military authority must prevail. Hahn inevitably complained to Lincoln, who responded, as he had to Banks a year earlier, with another uncharacteristically caustic letter, this time to Hurlbut. Marked *"Private"* and written after the election, Lincoln's letter defended his ten-percent plan and the Louisiana government to which it gave rise, and it equated support for the government and Louisiana's free-state constitution with loyalty, and opposition to them with secession. "Every advocate of slavery naturally desires to see blasted, and crushed, the liberty promised the black man by the new constitution," he argued. "But why Gen. Canby and Gen. Hurlbut should join on the same side is to me incomprehensible."

Both generals were stung by Lincoln's criticism and offered separate responses, with Hurlbut replying somewhat more defensively than did Canby. Perhaps recognizing he had gone overboard in possibly impugning his generals' motives, Lincoln penned a conciliatory letter to Canby. He nonetheless made it clear that he considered the Louisiana government entirely legitimate and a possible model for other seceded states to follow, and that he expected his commanders, while making every concession to military necessity, to assist rather than obstruct the work of reconstruction. "It is a worthy object to again get Louisiana into proper practical relations with the nation; and we can never finish this, if we never begin it," he insisted. "Much good work is already done, and surely nothing can be gained by throwing it away." This was neither the first nor last time Lincoln used this argument to defend Louisiana's government.[22]

In Tennessee, owing to military governor Andrew Johnson's selection as Lincoln's running mate, reconstruction and the presidential election intersected. The nomination of Johnson, a southern Democrat, was intended to attract northern and border-state Democrats to the Republican, or Union, ticket, but it exacerbated the conservative-radical divide among Tennessee Unionists. Conservatives condemned Lincoln's emancipation policy, with which Johnson was associated, and accused Johnson of plotting to tighten his stranglehold over the state. They formed a ticket that embraced both McClellan and, at least initially, the Democrats' Chicago platform, hoping ultimately to overthrow Johnson's administration, restore civilian government under their own control, and perhaps even return Tennessee to the Union with slavery intact. Although both factions agreed that the state should participate in the presidential election, each forwarded its own plan for doing so. Thus, conflict between Tennessee Unionists during the fall largely centered on the election and resulted in the inevitable appeal for presidential intervention.

In early September, Johnson's supporters dominated a loyalist convention held in Nashville to restore Tennessee to the Union and to organize a presidential election. After resolving that the state would participate in the election, the convention endorsed voting requirements much stricter than those of the ten-percent plan, including one provision requiring a prospective voter to swear to "oppose all armistices or negotiations for peace with rebels in arms." Later that month, Johnson publicly affirmed the work of the convention. And, once again, a group of conservative southern Unionists, fearful of being frozen out of the reconstruction process, protested to Lincoln. They drafted a petition, presented in person in mid-October, highlighting the incongruence between the leniency of Lincoln's loyalty oath and the harshness of Johnson's, and calling for Lincoln to revoke the latter. In short, they alleged that the convention and Johnson's proclamation amounted to an attempt to rig the presidential election in Tennessee, a plot with which Lincoln himself was said to be involved.

A petition so designed could hardly be expected to gain Lincoln's favor. Denying that he and Johnson had coordinated their actions in any way, Lincoln countered that no military reason compelled him to intervene in Tennessee and that, in any event, the president played no role in a state's presidential election. Several petitioners responded intemperately, charging that Johnson, as Lincoln's factotum, had unleashed a "reign of terror" in Tennessee and that Lincoln's course represented "a doctrine of despotism in 'irrepressible conflict' with the principles of public liberty." Others, however, realized that with Lincoln's reelection now all but certain, and with military operations still ongoing in the state, continued opposition to the administration was as unwise as it was counterproductive: it would only delay Tennessee's readmission to the Union and leave Johnson's supporters in control. Consequently, the McClellan campaign was abandoned, and some conservatives endorsed the Lincoln-Johnson ticket. The election took place in Tennessee, with Lincoln winning thirty thousand of the thirty-five thousand popular votes cast, but Congress did not count the state's electoral votes on the grounds that the election had not been legitimate.[23]

Responding to a serenade celebrating his reelection, Lincoln lauded the strength of American democracy. With its very existence at stake, the nation had conducted an election, demonstrating "that a people's government can sustain a national election, in the midst of a great civil war." "Until now it has not been known to the world that this was a possibility," he continued. "It shows also how *sound*, and how *strong* we still are." Lincoln took justifiable pride in the nation's and his own accomplishments. His defeat had been the Confederacy's last, best hope, but he won the endorsement of northern voters on a platform of prosecuting the war to final victory. And yet, as he had done on previous occasions of Union success, Lincoln reminded his audience that the war was far from over. "But the rebellion continues," he cautioned, "and now that the election is over, may not all, having a common interest, re-unite in a common effort, to save our common country?"

Implicit in Lincoln's remarks was the reality that eleven states had not participated in the election, since the large majority of their white populations did not consider themselves US citizens. And even in the four seceded states where Lincoln had installed loyal governments, no creditable presidential election had taken place. To judge even by the standards of his restorationist approach to reconstruction, Lincoln had little progress to report. No doubt, his reelection meant that the rebellion's defeat was a matter of time, notwithstanding Confederate determination to fight on. But in the eleven months since Lincoln had issued the ten-percent plan, none of the seceded states had been readmitted, and there was no telling when any of them would be. Despite the lack of progress on this front, several slave states had abolished slavery, thus commencing in earnest a reconstruction of southern society.

CHAPTER FOUR

"INTO PROPER PRACTICAL RELATIONS WITH THE UNION"

(November 1864–April 1865)

Abraham Lincoln's reelection sounded the Confederacy's death knell. In doing so, it also affirmed that his second term would be devoted to postwar reconstruction. Throughout the war, Lincoln had demonstrated his skill as military commander-in-chief, but with the end of hostilities in sight, his statesmanship—which itself had also been much in evidence—would now be put to the test. "The greatest question ever presented to practical statesmanship" is how Lincoln in 1863 had described the problem of reconstruction. Lincoln's words and actions during what would prove to be his final months provided only a glimpse of that statesmanship, as one of American history's greatest catastrophes denied Lincoln a second presidential term and the opportunity to shape the postwar world.

For Lincoln, long-term considerations pertaining to reconstruction were greatly complicated by more immediate concerns relating to the end of the war. Lacking any legitimacy, Confederate civilian authorities could not formally surrender, but Lincoln also warned his military leaders as the end neared that the terms of capitulation must avoid political matters. This problem might seem trivial in hindsight, but at the time it was not. In the aftermath of Confederate military defeat, maintaining law and order without recognizing Confederate civilian authority would be a delicate issue, especially since there was no telling how the Confederate political or military establishment or the southern white population at large would respond. For Lincoln and many others, guerilla warfare, a "scorched-earth" policy, or even race war were more than theoretical possibilities. Several observers noted Lincoln's concern over the South degenerating into lawlessness once Confederate authority collapsed. This concern led him into errors that could have had important consequences for reconstruction.

The war's final months also exacerbated for Lincoln the difficulty of urging Union supporters on to final victory while remaining open to peace overtures. Ever since Gettysburg and Vicksburg, Union military success had sparked calls for negotiations, and with Confederate defeat now ultimately certain, this pressure intensified. The closer the Union came to victory, the more Lincoln worried that northern resolve might weaken before victory had been achieved. At the same time, because Lincoln genuinely wanted the bloodshed over as quickly as possible, he was willing to entertain any offer that might achieve that end while also securing the goals of Union and emancipation. All other considerations could be delayed. The push for negotiations, combined with Lincoln's own desire for peace and fear of southern lawlessness, led to the secret conference at Hampton Roads, Virginia, in early February, 1865, and to Lincoln's ill-advised meeting in early April with the Confederate assistant secretary of war in Richmond. In truth, negotiations had no chance of success, but their failure reflected Lincoln's determination to continue the war so long as the Confederacy could field an army and its political leaders rejected his terms for peace.

The war's imminent end accentuated the tensions—even incompatibility—between the restorationist and reconstructionist dimensions of Lincoln's approach to reconstruction. The war's main goal for Lincoln had always been restoring federal authority over the seceded states. Yet this goal had also become subsumed within the larger process of reconstructing southern society, a process substantiated by congressional passage of the constitutional amendment abolishing slavery. The tensions between restoration and wholesale reconstruction were further reflected in congressional debate over various aspects of reconstruction, including whether the entire matter ought to be postponed until hostilities had ceased, and in conflicts in Virginia, Tennessee, Arkansas, and Louisiana, the seceded states undergoing reconstruction. These tensions were perhaps best epitomized by Lincoln himself in his last public address on April 11, in which he simultaneously employed restorationist language in defending the Louisiana government while also publicly endorsing black suffrage and articulating his hopes for a meaningful black freedom. The question of whether these goals were compatible seems not to have occurred to Lincoln.

Although Lincoln maintained that reconstruction had been going on all along, General Robert E. Lee's surrender at Appomattox marked a new departure. Despite the continuities in his approach to reconstruction, Lincoln clearly indicated before the end of the war, as he had done on previous occasions, that changed circumstances would require new approaches and ways of thinking. As early as December 1864, he hinted that his leniency toward former Confederates would not necessarily be continued once the war ended, and his last speech suggested a willingness to move even further than he already had on issues pertaining to emancipation and race. Lincoln did not have the opportunity to follow through on these intimations, but they demonstrate that his wartime reconstruction policies were not indicative of his intentions for the postwar world.

I

Following the election, the Union war machine rolled relentlessly forward. Grant's siege of Petersburg may have felt interminable, but it was only a matter of time before Lee's line broke and both Petersburg and Richmond fell. Sherman destroyed everything of value in and around Atlanta before embarking in mid-November on his "March to the Sea," which brought desolation to central Georgia and culminated in late December in the capture of Savannah. By late January, 1865, Sherman's army resumed its march north into the Carolinas. Meanwhile, Confederate general John Bell Hood, having abandoned Atlanta, took his army during the fall into northern Alabama and Tennessee before encountering catastrophic defeat at Nashville in mid-December. Despite these hard-fought Union gains, Confederates continued to mount fierce resistance, demonstrating

Lincoln's admonition that northern victory could not be taken for granted.

While remaining focused on the war, Lincoln began to think concretely about his second term. No president since Andrew Jackson had won reelection, and with his strong popular mandate, Lincoln was freer to shape his administration than he had been previously. None of the four new cabinet members was a major party leader or presidential aspirant, and they, along with holdovers William H. Seward (Department of State), Edwin M. Stanton (War), and Gideon Welles (Navy), made up a cabinet more personally loyal to Lincoln. The new cabinet also signified Lincoln's decreased concern with mediating Republican factionalism and his intent to shape his own administration's policies. Lincoln nominated former treasury secretary Salmon P. Chase as Chief Justice of the Supreme Court, as a reward for his support during the campaign and in expectation of his defense of administration wartime policy against possible legal challenge. The nomination was also intended to mollify Radical Republicans, with Congress convening in early December. Among the issues Congress was expected to consider, in addition to the constitutional amendment abolishing slavery, were a comprehensive reconstruction bill and the seating of members-elect from Louisiana and Arkansas.

A year earlier, the increasing prospects of Union success had prompted Lincoln in his annual message to Congress to advance a plan for reconstruction. Now, with the rebellion's defeat imminent, he used the address to spur Unionists on to victory while warning Confederates of possible changes to that plan. He first called attention to "important movements . . . to the effect of moulding society for durability in the Union." These included forming governments and framing free-state constitutions in Louisiana and Arkansas; similar though less successful developments in Tennessee, Kentucky, and Missouri; and abolishing slavery in Maryland. He then urged passage of the constitutional amendment abolishing slavery, which had failed earlier that year in the House, maintaining that the presidential election had served as a referendum on it and that the majority were clearly in favor. "It is the voice of the people now, for the first time, heard upon the question," he insisted. Moreover, the results of the congressional elections made passage inevitable, but because the Congress just elected would not convene for another year, it was all the more imperative that Congress approve the amendment during the current session.

Lincoln then observed that the election, though bitterly contested, revealed virtual unanimity in the loyal states for preserving the Union, and that the northern will to fight, along with its material advantages, meant the war could continue "indefinitely." Lincoln therefore tried to persuade Confederates to abandon the rebellion while they still could. In doing so, he also raised the possibility of altering his reconstruction policy, suggesting that continued resistance would affect his use of the pardoning power from which that policy was derived. He began this discussion with perhaps his most powerful repudiation of negotiations. Confederate president Jefferson Davis, Lincoln insisted, "would accept nothing short of severance of the Union—precisely what we will not and cannot give. His declarations to this effect are explicit and oft-repeated. He does not attempt to deceive us. He affords us no excuse to deceive ourselves. He cannot voluntarily reaccept the Union; we cannot voluntarily yield it. Between him and us the issue is distinct, simple, and inflexible. It is an issue which can only be tried by war, and decided by victory. If we yield, we are beaten; if the Southern people fail him, he is beaten. Either way, it would be the victory and defeat following war." Davis enjoyed no leeway, Lincoln maintained, but the southern people did, and they could end the war at any time by laying down their arms and submitting to federal authority. (Confederate measures such as conscription made this assertion dubious.) The war could not continue, and the people of the loyal states would not support it, once southern resistance ceased. "If questions should remain," Lincoln advised, "we would adjust them by the peaceful means of legislation, conference, courts, and votes, operating only in constitutional and lawful channels." Certain matters, Lincoln acknowledged, would no longer be under presidential control, but others, including pardons, would. "In what spirit and temper this control would be exercised can be fairly judged of by the past."

While this passage suggested Lincoln's intention to continue his policies toward Confederates, the next one did not. Referring to the ten-percent plan's pardoning provision, Lincoln remarked that "the door has been, for a full year, open to all"—or at least all who were free to choose. "It is still so open to all," but it would not be forever. "The time may come—probably will come—when public duty shall demand that it be closed; and that, in lieu, more rigorous measures than heretofore shall be adopted." Just as he had done with the preliminary emancipation proclamation two years earlier, Lincoln was offering Confederates both carrot and stick. Recognizing, however, that his argument—presenting submission to federal authority as "the only indispensable condition" to peace—could be interpreted as backtracking on emancipation, Lincoln immediately added that his policy on slavery remained unchanged. He employed his familiar refrain that he would neither retract nor modify the Emancipation Proclamation and no person freed during the war would be reenslaved. "In stating a single condition of peace," he concluded, "I mean simply to say that the war will cease on the part of the government, whenever it shall have ceased on the part of those who began it."

Lincoln was the master of ambiguity when it served his purpose, and his closing-the-door metaphor and warning of "more rigorous measures" was another instance. On the surface, one might reasonably conclude that Lincoln was considering wholesale changes to his reconstruction policy. Yet it might also be argued that Lincoln was discussing not reconstruction in general but the specific issue of pardon and amnesty, and that "more rigorous measures" referred to neither the conditions of state readmission nor the consequences of emancipation. Either reading is plausible. Lincoln no doubt threatened to revoke his pardoning policy in order to induce white southerners to abandon the Confederacy. Still, because Lincoln had based the ten-percent plan so firmly on the presidential pardon, it would not be implausible to suppose that changes to the latter might result in corresponding changes to the former. Perhaps more importantly, the language in which Lincoln framed this discussion, though ambiguous, was strikingly similar to that which he had used in reference to emancipation during spring and summer 1862, when he was considering the proclamation and preparing the public for it. Clemency was still available, Lincoln was saying, but it would not be indefinitely. Implicit is the warning that Confederates who continued armed resistance to federal authority would suffer the consequences once the rebellion had been suppressed. The point is admittedly speculative, but Lincoln may have been preparing the public for a future distinction between Confederates who voluntarily resumed their allegiance to the Union, however late in the day, and those who resisted to the bitter end.[2]

Although enacting reconstruction legislation—and having a policy toward the seceded states in place when the war ended—was an important objective of the congressional session, the immediate priority was passing the amendment abolishing slavery. Lincoln had remained noncommittal and had made no attempt to influence congressional action on the amendment the previous spring, when it had passed in the Senate by the necessary two-thirds margin but failed to do so in the House. In the following weeks, however, he had come to support the amendment, no doubt out of genuine commitment but perhaps also to outflank the Frémont-Radical threat. As the June 1864 Republican-Union convention approached, he had clearly approved of including the amendment in the party's platform. Now, in addition to urging Congress to pass the amendment, he led a major lobbying effort to win approval. Republicans would reliably vote in favor, but to gain a two-thirds majority, several Democratic and border-state representatives, almost all of whom had opposed the amendment, would have to change their votes. Eventually, fierce executive pressure brought enough of them around to enable House passage in late January. Notwithstanding allegations that Lincoln cut political deals to gain the needed votes, what is certain, as Eric Foner has observed, is that he intervened more directly in the legislative process on this matter than on any other of his presidency. So satisfied was Lincoln with the victory that he signed the congressional resolution sending the amendment to the states for ratification, even though his signature was unnecessary. Responding to a serenade, he called the amendment "a King's cure for all the evils," since it eliminated the war's "original disturbing cause" and rectified the limitations and legal uncertainties of the Emancipation Proclamation. "It winds the whole thing up," Lincoln proclaimed, congratulating the nation for "this great moral victory."[3]

Despite Lincoln's claims for its finality, the Thirteenth Amendment in the years to come would raise as many questions as it answered, including several with immediate implications for reconstruction. The amendment definitively ended gradual emancipation, long a staple of American thinking, but it did not bar compensating slaveholders. (The Fourteenth Amendment did so in 1868.) Debate on the amendment also addressed but did not resolve the question of whether or not the seceded states would be included in determining the number of states needed for ratification. With thirty-six states in the Union, including the eleven seceded states, twenty-seven were required. Exclusion of the seceded states would facilitate ratification, but it could also be used to question the ratification process and even to recognize the Confederacy, whereas their inclusion would have the opposite effects. Although the latter position, which Lincoln supported, eventually prevailed, it remained unclear whether ratification would be required for readmission to the Union. This question was especially pertinent, since, given the uncertain status of Lincoln's southern governments, the eleven seceded states could block ratification. At this point the issue of what role the seceded states might play in incorporating into the constitution a principle that had prompted their secession in the first place was far from settled.

These and other issues relating to reconstruction surfaced during an episode that formed a subplot to the Thirteenth Amendment and ranks among the strangest of Lincoln's presidency: the secret conference between Lincoln, Seward, and Confederate officials at Hampton Roads, Virginia, in early February. Lincoln had been besieged throughout the war by would-be diplomats, and the Confederacy's imminent demise sparked others. Among these, Francis Blair Sr., leader of the powerful family from Missouri and Maryland, proposed meeting with Jefferson Davis in order to effect an armistice and create a joint military mission to evict the French regime from Mexico. His doubts notwithstanding, Lincoln allowed Blair to travel to Richmond in early January to meet with Davis. The Confederacy appeared to be falling apart, dissent was rife, and the national government had even begun considering arming slaves. Davis expressed interest in a conference "with a view to secure peace to the two countries," phrasing that Lincoln obviously deemed unacceptable. Lincoln therefore sent Blair back to Richmond with word that he would consider meeting informally with Confederate representatives for the purpose of restoring peace to "our one common country." As Lincoln had put the matter in his annual address, and as these two communications demonstrated, there was little to discuss. Both sides wanted peace, however, and even Grant was open to a possible meeting.[4]

Although Lincoln had become amenable by late January to an informal conference, rumors of the proposed meeting jeopardized the Thirteenth Amendment during final debate. Lincoln justifiably worried that even the hint of peace would give wavering Democrats an excuse to retract their support, resorting to the specious but intractable argument that Republican emancipation policy was the main obstacle to peace. When Ohio Republican James Ashley, who was instrumental in garnering support for the amendment, asked Lincoln to verify that negotiations were not in the offing, Lincoln famously replied that, to his knowledge, no peace commissioners were in Washington or likely to be. This sophistry helped salvage the amendment, but it also kept alive the proposed conference, which Lincoln probably would have preferred to scuttle.

On the very day of the vote on the amendment, Lincoln outlined to Seward his conditions for the meeting. They included his by-now familiar articulation of Union war goals: restoration of the national authority over the states, no receding by the executive on wartime measures regarding slavery, and no armistice short of a complete end to the war and disbanding of Confederate forces. He pledged to consider all other matters "in a spirit of sincere liberality." Three days later, on the morning of February 3, Lincoln joined Seward in meeting with three Confederate officials: vice president Alexander H. Stephens, assistant secretary of war John A. Campbell, and former secretary of state and senator from Virginia Robert M. T. Hunter. A former Georgia Whig who had opposed secession until his state seceded, Stephens had served in Congress with Lincoln, and both men genuinely respected each other.

From the firing on Fort Sumter, Lincoln had maintained that so long as the seceded states forcibly resisted federal authority, there could be no negotiated settlement. Now, he was meeting, however informally, with representatives of a government he deemed illegitimate. The conference took place on a steamer anchored off Hampton Roads, near the mouth of the James River, and it lasted several hours. Since no notes or minutes were kept, there is some disagreement over what was discussed. Following some preliminary chatter, the meeting commenced in earnest with Lincoln being asked what terms he would offer the Confederate states for returning to the Union. He responded that once resistance had ceased the states would quickly resume their practical relations with the Union—his standard formulation—and he would exercise leniency in issuing pardons and restoring property. However, he also insisted, as he always had, that no discussion of terms could even begin until resistance to federal authority had ceased. When reminded that, during the English civil wars of the mid-seventeenth century, Charles I had negotiated with rebels amidst hostilities, Lincoln famously retorted that all he remembered about Charles I was that "he lost his head in the end."

The meeting then turned to the slavery question. According to Stephens, Lincoln recommended that Georgia withdraw from the Confederacy and ratify the Thirteenth Amendment with the provision that it not become operative for five years. Stephens also claimed that when Lincoln was asked about the status of slaves in the Confederate states who, though legally freed by the Emancipation Proclamation, had not gained their freedom, he responded that, because the proclamation had been a war measure, it would become inoperative once the war ended, and it would apply only to slaves who had actually gained their freedom while it had been in effect. Stephens's first claim is hardly creditable, but the second is at least plausible in light of Lincoln's insistence, according to Seward, that ratification of the Thirteenth Amendment was inevitable. Lincoln seems to have been indicating that the seceded states would participate in the process of ratifying the amendment, even if he did not specify that ratification would be a condition for readmission. Yet, because all the loyal states would not necessarily ratify the amendment, it would need approval from at least several Confederate states. Thus, Lincoln may have considered ratification an eventuality because he envisioned requiring it of the seceded states in exchange for leniency on other issues. Even the appearance of Lincoln casting doubt on the Emancipation Proclamation, as Stephens claimed, must be understood within the context of the Thirteenth Amendment, which would obviate all questions concerning wartime slavery measures. But Lincoln could only consider ratification inevitable, as Seward claimed, with approval from the Confederate states. Such approval, in turn, would have to be secured by either a requirement or some incentive.

Lincoln may have envisaged such an incentive when he mentioned, again according to Stephens, the possibility of compensating slaveholders. Gradual, compensated emancipation had long been essential to Lincoln's thought, and while gradualism were now dead, compensation might still induce Confederates to give up the fight. Three years earlier, the proposal to compensate border-state slaveholders for what Lincoln then claimed was slavery's inevitable demise had gone nowhere, but at that point Confederate defeat was hardly imminent. Now the situation was very different, and the Thirteenth Amendment did not prohibit compensation. Stephens's account gains credibility on this point (and, some historians argue, on the others) from the fact that Lincoln, almost immediately after returning to Washington, drew up a compensated emancipation proposal that he discussed with his cabinet. Dated February 5, 1865, it proposed that a sum of four hundred million dollars be made available to the slaveholding states on condition that the rebellion entirely cease by April 1, when one-half of the sum would be disbursed. The rest would be paid provided that the Thirteenth Amendment were ratified by the requisite number of states by July 1. Lincoln was undoubtedly attempting to exploit divisions between the Confederate leadership, which refused to capitulate, and the southern white population, especially slaveholders who might gain something by ending the war quickly. Moreover, although he was not explicitly requiring the seceded states to ratify the amendment, he was nonetheless linking Confederate surrender to ratification. The plan contained a certain logic, but the cabinet unanimously opposed it on both practical and philosophical grounds: it would never pass Congress, especially on such short notice; it was unduly conciliatory, and might even be construed as weakness; and, as Lincoln himself had always maintained, until resistance ended, the rebellion could be put down only by force. "You are all against me," he reluctantly concluded, abandoning the idea.

The peace conference had been a poorly kept secret, and Lincoln eventually submitted the relevant documentation to Congress (excluding his compensation proposal), observing that it "ended without result." This characterization was not entirely correct, for the result was just not the one he had hoped for. Some Republicans criticized Lincoln for undertaking the mission, but most others applauded his commitment to reunion and emancipation while demonstrating flexibility on other issues. Lincoln always maintained that there was nothing to be gained from talking, but his agreeing to do so at this point showed his desire for peace. He was even willing, at this late date, to recognize slaveholders' property rights and compensate them if doing so would end the bloodshed. Lincoln had always subscribed to these two ideas, so he was saying nothing new. Yet now he was bargaining from a position of strength, and he was under no obligation to demonstrate magnanimity—except insofar as it might bring peace to "our one common country."

II

Even as these events were unfolding, the second session of the Thirty-Eighth Congress, which met from December 1864 to early March, 1865, revisited various matters relating to reconstruction. These included a comprehensive bill governing readmission of the seceded states, legislation addressing the consequences of emancipation, and Lincoln's Louisiana and Arkansas governments. Deliberation on these issues, in turn, was shaped by developments in the southern states. Almost every wartime congressional session had considered reconstruction legislation, and the one time Congress reached consensus, with the Wade-Davis bill, Lincoln vetoed it. Now, with Lincoln's reelection decided and the war's end imminent, Congress would try again.

As before, the myriad issues arising from reconstruction led to complicated legislative wrangling. In addition to the familiar partisan, factional, and constitutional divisions, there was now disagreement over whether the impending end of the war meant Congress should enact a comprehensive reconstruction bill or whether it should defer action until it could gauge the white southern response to defeat. Although legislative deferral also meant surrendering the initiative to the executive branch, most Republicans considered this course acceptable in light of Lincoln's electoral mandate. Actions taken at this point were based on the assumption not of Lincoln's being assassinated in a few short weeks but of his fulfilling a second presidential term.

Congress's final wartime reconstruction measure resembled the Wade-Davis bill in key ways and thus presented another alternative to Lincoln's policy. Introduced in mid-December, 1864, by House Republican James Ashley, who also shepherded the Thirteenth Amendment to final passage, the Ashley bill, like Wade-Davis, required the seceded states to abolish slavery and outlined the process for their restoration to the Union. Both bills also embraced the attorney general's 1862 ruling that considered free black people to be American citizens, but the Ashley bill went further by requiring "all male citizens" to be enrolled as voters and jurors. Although Ashley's bill did not define citizenship or otherwise address black civil rights, its black suffrage requirement clearly put it at odds with the ten-percent plan. At the same time, the bill struck a compromise with the president by recognizing his Louisiana government while excluding it from the black suffrage provision.[5]

The bill emerged from what Republican congressional leaders, including Massachusetts senator Charles Sumner, believed was an understanding with Lincoln: Congress would recognize the Louisiana government in exchange for presidential support for a reconstruction bill requiring the other seceded states to adopt equality before the law and black suffrage. Whether such an understanding had been reached was debated at the time and has been since. In a mid-December meeting with General Nathaniel P. Banks, who spent the entire fall in Washington and the northeast lobbying Congress and drumming up support for the Louisiana government, Lincoln is said to have opposed the bill's black suffrage provision. According to John Hay, Lincoln's secretary who had also been present, Lincoln approved of the bill "with the exception of one or two things which he thought rather calculated to conceal a feature which might be objectionable to some. The first was that under the provisions of that bill negroes would be made jurors & voters under the temporary governments."[6]

Lincoln's words could be read in at least two ways. He might have been expressing his own opposition to the bill's black suffrage provision, thus indicating that the states should control their voting requirements. Conversely, he might have been stating objectively that such a provision would never get through Congress. The latter reading is plausible, but most contemporaries understood the former to represent Lincoln's position, and Ashley's bill was diluted to restrict voting to loyal white males and black Union veterans. Yet as debate dragged on through January and most of February, the bill was further revised until it became clear that Congress could not reach agreement. With the session winding down and the end of the war at hand, it was deemed best to defer action on the issue until the next Congress, which was not scheduled to convene until December 1865, since other matters required attention.

As Congress worked on a reconstruction plan in late 1864 and early 1865, Unionists in Arkansas, Tennessee, and Louisiana continued to reorganize state governments under Lincoln's policy. In all three cases, though more so in the latter two, both advocates and detractors of the ten-percent plan could point to evidence to substantiate their viewpoints. In Arkansas, local elections were held, and the state legislature met and attempted to address the many problems war had brought to the state. Perhaps the most important development was the state legislature's replacing of US senator-elect William M. Fishback, whose selection had sparked so much controversy, with William D. Snow, in hopes of increasing congressional support for seating Arkansas's representatives.[7]

In Tennessee, where military affairs had repeatedly hampered reconstruction, Unionists hoped finally to reorganize the state before Lincoln's reinauguration. Led by military governor and now vice president-elect Andrew Johnson, they called for a Unionist meeting to be held in Nashville, which, though delayed by Hood's fall military campaign, convened in early January. After considerable debate over its actual purpose, the assembly, with Johnson playing a key role, approved constitutional amendments abolishing slavery and nullifying the secession ordinance that would go to the voters for ratification. No provisions were made for black civil rights, which were left to the state legislature. The assembly set an election on the amendments for February and another in March for governor and state legislature, and it restricted voting to those who had qualified for the presidential election, thus excluding many former Confederates. It also nominated William G. "Parson" Brownlow—the famed minister, newspaper editor, and radical Unionist whom Confederate authorities had nearly hanged earlier in the war for his loyalism—for governor, and it named a committee to appeal to Lincoln to issue a proclamation declaring Tennessee to be no longer in rebellion. Lincoln was sympathetic to the request when he met with the committee in early February, but he did not issue the proclamation, largely due to the Confederate forces in western Tennessee.

After the assembly, Johnson informed Lincoln of its actions, explicitly hoping for Tennessee's exclusion from Ashley's reconstruction bill. He also proposed remaining in Tennessee until the April instillation of the state's reconstructed government, though doing so would entail missing his own inauguration as vice president. Citing security concerns, Lincoln urged Johnson to be in Washington for the inaugural. In the campaign for the amendments and new state government, conservative Unionists charged that the assembly had exceeded its authority in drawing up constitutional amendments and had violated the spirit of Lincoln's lenient reconstruction policy in nominating the divisive Brownlow. Radical Unionists, by contrast, campaigned enthusiastically, hoping a large turnout would justify the state's readmission. With former Confederates barred from the elections and conservatives boycotting them, the constitutional amendment abolishing slavery won overwhelming approval in February, and in March Brownlow was elected governor while radical Unionists secured control of the legislature. Although turnout was down from the presidential election, more than ten percent of the number of voters in 1860 had participated in the state elections, and the new government prepared to assume office.[8]

Reconstruction appeared to be moving ahead in Tennessee, but such was not the case in Louisiana. During the fall, the moderate

Banks-Hahn faction of the Free State organization had dominated elections for the state legislature and US House of Representatives, while the civilian government, despite Banks's absence, managed to deflect the hostility of Union military authorities, radicals, and ultraconservatives. Banks's expected return in early 1865 was repeatedly delayed by his work in Congress, and he eventually returned only after Lincoln's assassination. Whatever his faults, Banks's extended absence no doubt adversely affected the situation in Louisiana. In October, the state legislature elected R. Cutler King and Charles Smith to the US Senate, and their attempted seating in early 1865 would mark the major test of Lincoln's Louisiana government. In January, meanwhile, the legislature elected Governor Michael Hahn to replace Smith, whose term in the Thirty-Eighth Congress was due to expire in March. (Thus, Hahn was elected to the Thirty-Ninth Congress *before* the Thirty-Eighth Congress had decided whether to seat King and Smith.) Although Hahn's status as senator-elect was provisional (he would not be seated when the Thirty-Ninth Congress convened in December 1865), he resigned as governor in early March and was replaced by Lieutenant-Governor J. Madison Wells, a conservative Unionist. With Banks away, Wells immediately began replacing Hahn's appointments with ultraconservatives and former Confederates.

Racial matters in late 1864 and early 1865 also worried critics of Louisiana's government. Pressed by Hahn and Union military authorities, the state legislature ratified the Thirteenth Amendment in February, though only after what seemed excessive debate. Moreover, it rejected every other measure, however symbolic, that even appeared to advance racial equality, including bills abolishing the antebellum slave code, permitting interracial marriage, and extending the vote to black Union army veterans or to mulattoes who were Union veterans or who met property or literacy requirements. The legislature also rejected compulsory elementary education, despite the importance Lincoln placed on education for black freedom. Neither did the draconian features of wartime free labor under military auspices inspire confidence. These developments were especially disappointing to the emerging coalition of free people of color and former slaves, who in January held a convention of the National Equal Rights League in

New Orleans advocating racial equality. Lincoln's entire approach to reconstruction had been intended to entice Confederates to resume their former allegiance, even offering them a chance to shape the postwar social order if they did so. But Louisiana affairs were already demonstrating the pitfalls of granting white southerners, even Unionists, a monopoly on political power.[9]

Even as developments in the southern states were unfolding, Congress grappled with other aspects of reconstruction as the session wound down in late February and early March. Although the supposed agreement between Lincoln and Republican congressional leaders collapsed with the failure of Ashley's bill, defenders of Lincoln's reconstruction policy hoped Congress might still seat the members-elect from Louisiana and Arkansas before adjourning. The seating question had originally been linked to the Ashley bill, but once the latter's defeat became clear, defenders and critics of Lincoln's policy mobilized over the former. As congressional committees examined the matter in January and early February, the prospects of seating the claimants initially appeared promising. Attention focused on the Senate, since it directly involved the state governments, and most Republicans probably favored seating the claimants. However, a "strange-bedfellows" alliance of Radical Republicans, including Sumner, and conservative Democrats came together and filibustered to prevent the seating. With several critical measures still to consider, and with a number of Lincoln's supporters hesitant to act hastily, the Senate voted to postpone the question until the next Congress. The Ashley bill's outcome may have been seen as a victory for Lincoln, but this was a defeat. The members of Louisiana's and Arkansas's delegations were dismayed, though Lincoln vowed to support the governments, and most congressional Republicans viewed the result as a postponement of reconstruction rather than as a major setback for Lincoln. The action even made sense, since Congress had effectively handed reconstruction over to Lincoln as the end of the war neared.[10]

As had been the case with the Wade-Davis bill, the disagreement between Lincoln and congressional Republicans, the Radicals in particular, over the Louisiana-Arkansas governments did not amount to an irreparable breach. Lincoln and Sumner continued to maintain cordial personal relations. Lincoln may have felt secure in his position as his second term dawned, but the Radicals were likewise confident that Lincoln would eventually come around to their position on black civil rights and postwar reconstruction, as he had on so many other issues.

Indeed, even as Ashley's bill and Lincoln's governments were going down to defeat, congressional Republicans and Lincoln agreed on a measure that would have profound repercussions for postwar reconstruction: establishing the Bureau of Refugees, Freedmen, and Abandoned Lands. An agency within the War Department intended to oversee the transition from slavery to freedom, the "Freedmen's Bureau" assumed responsibility for "all subjects" relating to freedmen. It was specifically authorized to take control of abandoned farms and plantations in possession of the US government, and to make lands from them available for rental and eventual sale in forty-acre plots to former slaves and loyal white refugees. The amount of land in question (less than one million acres) would hardly have initiated widespread land redistribution in the South, but the legislation would potentially have made land available to thousands of freed families, and it might have created the precedent for further land reform. Although originally envisioned as a temporary agency, to last for only one year after the war's end, the bureau represented a major expansion of federal authority. Congress passed the Freedmen's Bureau bill as the session ended, and Lincoln immediately signed it. Beyond that, he took no other action and seems to have expressed no opinion on the bureau. (He also signed legislation creating the "Freedman's Bank.") Lincoln had already become keenly solicitous of the former slaves as laborers, and he had begun to envision an interventionist role for the federal government in creating a free-labor South. What the bureau might have become under Lincoln's authority is one of American history's "what-ifs," even though Lincoln was decidedly unsympathetic to land confiscation. The hostility of Lincoln's successor Andrew Johnson toward the bureau would play a critical role in his break with congressional Republicans in 1866 and in the adopting of what would come to be known as "Radical Reconstruction."

Historians have long debated the relations between Lincoln and the Radical Republicans. Some emphasize the tensions between them, usually in order to lift up Lincoln's moderation or conservatism, whereas others focus on their ability to work together, thus highlighting Lincoln's pragmatism or even his radical proclivities. Genuine ideological differences no doubt separated Lincoln and the Radicals, but so long as the war continued, securing the twin goals of Union and emancipation overrode any differences between them; and so long as Lincoln and all Republicans faced a viable foe in the northern Democratic Party, as Eric L. McKitrick has observed, the dictates of both nation and party compelled them to work together.[11]

And yet, notwithstanding their similarities, perhaps the most significant difference between Lincoln and the Radicals involved the larger connection between the war and reconstruction. For the Radicals, the two were distinct, and the war of conquest had to end before the reconstruction of southern society could begin. For Lincoln, the two had always been inseparable, even though his vision of reconstruction had evolved from restoring states to reconstructing southern society. What the war's end would have meant for these contrasting modes of thought, and for relations between Lincoln and the Radicals, remains a matter of speculation. The need for party unity no doubt would have forced Lincoln and congressional Republicans, including the Radicals, to agree on policy. Likewise, on matters of genuine principle, the differences between Lincoln and the Radicals were often more apparent than real. As Lincoln had said to Sumner on emancipation in late 1861, the "only difference" between them was "a month or six weeks in time." Even if this difference had increased by early 1865, it still remained less than that between Republicans and northern Democrats, or between most northerners and most white southerners.[12]

III

Bridging the divide between northerners and white southerners after the war would dominate Lincoln's second term, as he made clear at his second inauguration. Lincoln's second inaugural address justifiably ranks among his greatest works—along with the Gettysburg

Address—and among the most important documents in American history. The address's religious overtones and poetic language, as some contemporaries observed, may have made it an unusual official state document, but it also represented one of Lincoln's most eloquent expressions of the war's transcendent meaning. Even as it attempted to reckon with America's past, the address also looked to the future, to a nation reunited and rid of slavery.

The phrase "With malice toward none; with charity for all" is often cited as evidence of Lincoln's intended leniency toward former Confederates after the war. Reconciliation and forgiveness were no doubt central themes to the address, just as they had underpinned Lincoln's approach to the war. Virtually everything Lincoln had done since Fort Sumter had attempted to induce Confederates to resume their former allegiance. Nonetheless, while reconciliation was integral to the second inaugural, Lincoln was not so much absolving the South for slavery or the war as he was assigning to the rest of the nation its share of responsibility. Less intent on forbearance for the white South, Lincoln was instead reminding all white Americans that they collectively bore guilt for the wrong of slavery, and that war was the price of redemption. Furthermore, as Eric Foner has observed, by pinpointing slavery as "the cause of the war"; by describing the war's results, including the end of slavery, as both "fundamental" and "astounding"; and by referring to the slaves as part of the "whole" population of the country, Lincoln was indicating that mercy for former Confederates would have to be accompanied by justice for the former slaves. He may have wanted, as he famously put it, to "bind up the nation's wounds," but national reconciliation, however desirable, would have to be part of a larger objective: that of achieving "a just, and a lasting peace." It has been observed that peace and justice cannot always coexist: an ostensible "peace" has often been predicated on injustice, whereas the pursuit of justice throughout history has at times required a resort to violence. For Lincoln, any peace following the war would have to be more just than the antebellum peace, which had been rooted in the violence and injustice of slavery.[13]

The pursuit of justice was still for the future; victory and peace were imminent by the time of Lincoln's address. Sherman was completing his march of destruction through South Carolina and preparing to move into North Carolina. There, Confederate general Joseph E. Johnston had managed to assemble several thousand troops near Raleigh in hopes of linking up with Lee at Petersburg, but this initiative had virtually no chance of success. Meanwhile, the last Confederate strongholds on the Atlantic coast had already fallen. It would only be weeks before Lee, whose lines were stretched to the breaking point, faced complete encirclement. The Confederate project was ending.

As the end neared, Lincoln had to balance his desire for peace against his fear of allowing victory to slip away. He therefore urged his generals to maintain the pressure while instructing them to remain open to peace overtures. Yet even this approach entailed risk. In early March, Lee contacted Grant for the purpose of holding a "military convention" that might end hostilities. Grant forwarded the communication to Washington, and Lincoln was initially amenable to the idea until Secretary of War Stanton warned that Lee's message could be construed as containing a political component. Lincoln then instructed Stanton to inform Grant to have no conference with Lee unless "for the capitulation of [his] army" or a minor military point. Grant was further advised "not to decide, discuss, or confer upon any political question." These "the President holds in his own hands," Stanton added, "and will submit them to no military conferences or conventions." Grant was told "to press to the utmost, your military advantages."[14]

Such instructions seemed straightforward. However, because Lincoln had always thought of the war and reconstruction as inseparable, his wish to allow for lenient surrender terms, so as to encourage Confederates to abandon the fight, could potentially make it difficult to distinguish between military and political questions. How difficult became evident following Lincoln's meeting in late March with his military leadership at City Point, Virginia. Hoping to escape the political cauldron of Washington, visit the troops (which he often did), and confer with his generals, Lincoln decided to join Grant outside Petersburg. He arrived on March 23 and remained near the front for the next two weeks, returning to Washington only when Secretary of State Seward suffered serious injury in a carriage accident. During March 27–28, Lincoln met with Grant, Sherman (up from North Carolina), and Admiral David Porter to discuss the impending Confederate surrender.[15]

The meeting later resulted in a well-known painting, but its most important consequence for reconstruction was what Sherman took from it. During the meeting, according to Sherman, Lincoln expressed his wish to end the war as quickly as possible and prevent unnecessary suffering. Yet also concerned lest the defeated South descend into anarchy, Lincoln instructed Grant and Sherman to offer generous surrender terms in hopes of inducing the Confederate armies to disband and the soldiers to return home. Sherman later claimed that Lincoln distinctly authorized him to assure the governor and people of North Carolina that, as soon as hostilities ceased, "they would at once be guaranteed all their rights as citizens of a common country," and that, to avoid disorder, Lincoln would recognize the state governments. Three weeks later, following Lee's surrender and Lincoln's assassination, Joseph E. Johnston surrendered to Sherman. Not only did the capitulation offer generous terms, but it also addressed the very political questions Lincoln had undoubtedly instructed his generals to avoid. They included presidential recognition of the southern state governments once their officials had taken the necessary loyalty oaths, adjudication by the US Supreme Court where rival state governments existed, the establishment of federal courts in the South, and the restoration of all political and property rights to individuals, without the essential proviso excepting slaves. Once these terms became known, they resulted in a hailstorm of criticism against Sherman, and President Johnson rejected the surrender and sent Grant to North Carolina to instruct Sherman to impose the same terms on Johnston that Grant had imposed on Lee.

It is difficult to believe that Lincoln had instructed Sherman as Sherman later claimed. At the very least, Sherman would have had no reason to consult with a state governor in securing the surrender of Confederate military forces. The terms he originally gave Johnston also contradicted almost entirely Lincoln's policy regarding the governments of seceded states. Lincoln may have discussed with his generals some of the issues Sherman included in his agreement with

Johnston, but Sherman, perhaps in his desire to end the conflict definitively, especially in the volatile aftermath of Lincoln's assassination, undoubtedly misunderstood Lincoln's intent. Grant had no problem distinguishing between military and political questions, and, following Sherman's blunder, no Union general repeated his mistake as the Confederacy's western forces continued to surrender.

Nonetheless, Sherman's mistake becomes understandable when measured against Lincoln's own logic. Given his desperation to end the war, his determination to prevent lawlessness in the South, and his eagerness to restore the seceded states to the Union, Lincoln created the preconditions for his military commanders to venture into political terrain. Neither could he entirely avoid dealing with Confederate civilian authorities, either to end hostilities or to maintain order once they had ceased. In a sense, Lincoln was confronting the challenge that victors in war have historically faced: that of having to incorporate their foes' political and military structure, if only to prevent chaos. To be sure, civil authority within the seceded states had existed independent of the rebellion, and civil officials' cooperation would be essential once the Confederate military had been disbanded. Despite Lincoln's adamance in seeing reconstruction in practical rather than theoretical terms, his adherence to the legal fiction that the seceded states had never left the Union effectively meant that all Confederate authority was illegitimate, potentially leaving the South devoid of basic government. State and local officials in the seceded states would have to be recognized, or federal military authorities would have to assume all their responsibilities until new governments were established, or the South would descend into disorder. Sherman undoubtedly viewed the last option as unthinkable, the second as undesirable, and the first as unavoidable.

Sherman also later claimed that he had simply followed the example of Lincoln, who held what turned out to be an ill-advised meeting in Richmond in early April with Confederate assistant secretary of war John A. Campbell, one of the participants in February's Hampton Roads conference. It was during Lincoln's two-week visit to the front that federal forces finally broke through Lee's line at Petersburg, forcing the evacuation of that city and of Richmond, which fell on April 3. Over the following two days, Lincoln conducted his famous tour of the Confederate capital, the black population of which hailed him as a veritable savior. Although Lee's army was heading toward its date with destiny at Appomattox, no one could anticipate when he might capitulate. Lincoln thus met with Campbell, the only high-ranking Confederate official still in the city, to discuss Virginia's possible withdrawal from the Confederacy. The meeting and its aftermath would provoke much opposition from Lincoln's own cabinet and party, as his desire to end the war potentially jeopardized postwar reconstruction.[16]

Following a preliminary meeting on April 4, Lincoln and Campbell met the next morning to discuss ending Virginia's participation in the rebellion. Also in attendance was General Godfrey Weitzel, the federal military commander in Richmond. Lincoln's "indispensible terms" for peace were identical to those he had presented at Hampton Roads: restoration of the national authority, no receding from wartime measures on slavery, and complete disbanding of Confederate military forces, along with a pledge to consider all other questions "in a spirit of sincere liberality." Once again employing carrot and stick, Lincoln also promised to return any previously confiscated property, excepting slaves, to the people of any state that withdrew from the Confederacy, while further stipulating that, should resistance continue, such property would be used to bear the war's additional cost. Campbell, for his part, admitted slavery "to be defunct," and he indicated, according to Weitzel, that "if amnesty could be offered[,] the rebel army would dissolve and all the States return." Lincoln did not promise amnesty, but he pledged to use the pardon to "save any repentant sinner from hanging." Campbell also proposed "a military convention, to cover appearances," in ending the conflict. Despite the potential for agreement, the absence of any Confederate national official with authority to surrender underscored the problem of dismantling a government that officially did not exist.

With Lincoln hoping to hasten Virginia's withdrawal from the Confederacy, and with Campbell perhaps hoping to secure the state's timely restoration to the Union, the two men tentatively agreed on a plan, one that Lincoln himself had evidently been pondering. It called for Lincoln to allow the members of Virginia's Confederate legislature to meet in Richmond and vote to withdraw the state from the Confederacy. The plan entailed obvious risk. It violated Lincoln's steadfast refusal to recognize Confederate authority and potentially undermined the legitimacy of Virginia's Unionist government. Acknowledging Confederate authority in order to secure a state's withdrawal from the rebellion could be justified as a necessity. But calling into question the Pierpont government could invalidate not only the creation of West Virginia but also Virginia's abolition of slavery and its ratification of the Thirteenth Amendment. It could also be used to challenge Lincoln's other reconstruction efforts. Still, the proposal had the one advantage, which Lincoln must have found irresistible, of possibly removing Virginia's officers and men, including Robert E. Lee, from the rebellion.

Given the proposal's sensitivity, Lincoln did not agree to it during the meeting with Campbell but returned to army headquarters at City Point, where he labored over its wording. The next day, April 6, he issued a carefully crafted order to Weitzel, allowing "the gentlemen who have acted as the Legislature of Virginia, in support of the rebellion," to assemble in Richmond and "take measures to withdraw the Virginia troops, and other support from resistance to the General government." The legislators were guaranteed protection so long as they engaged in no action hostile to the United States; were they to attempt such action, they were to be given reasonable time to disperse, after which they would be arrested. Lincoln instructed Weitzel to show the order to Campbell but otherwise keep it secret, and he informed Grant of the situation, assuring him that it was not to affect military operations.

Whatever benefit Lincoln hoped to derive from the plan, he gained none. To the contrary, it backfired. During the next three days, about a dozen legislators gathered in Richmond but took no action. Worse, Campbell took a more expansive view of Lincoln's order than Lincoln had intended. Writing to Weitzel on April 7, Campbell called for a military armistice, proposed negotiations between the United States and the governments of Virginia and South Carolina, and even questioned the validity of the Emancipation Proclamation. More broadly, Campbell viewed the Confederacy as a duly constituted government that had made no arrangements for its own demise. "The obstacles to an immediate accommodation arise [from the] condition of the Confederate Government and nature of the questions involved [in] the war," he wrote. "The Confederate Government has made no provision [for] the possibility of its failure. Its functionaries don't understand how [they] can negotiate for the subversion or overthrow of their [Government]. All the powers of negotiations are in the hands of the [President], and he is not willing to employ them for such [a] result. . . . Thus while reflecting persons are convinced that the [cause] of the Confederate States can't be achieved, and they are predisposed [to] an adjustment, there is a great difficulty in obtaining an [acknowledgment] of this conviction from a legally constituted authority."

Clearly, this was not what Lincoln had had in mind. Moreover, despite Lincoln's wish to keep the matter secret, word almost immediately slipped out. Weitzel further compounded the problem by publishing in the Richmond newspapers a call for the legislature to assemble in accordance with Lincoln's guidelines—on the very day a congressional delegation was in the city. By the time Lincoln returned to Washington on the afternoon of April 9, owing to Seward's accident, he was met by jubilation over Lee's anticipated surrender and Republican anger over his Virginia proposal.

Whereas Campbell had pinpointed Lincoln's dilemma of trying to induce Confederates to capitulate without recognizing their authority, Lee's surrender on April 9 ought to have rendered the point moot. But it did not. During the next several days, Lincoln continued to defend the plan—insisting that provisions had to be made to prevent lawlessness—even as he reaffirmed his support for Virginia's Unionist government. For their part, leading Republicans and the entire cabinet opposed the plan, expressing grave reservations over its implicit recognition of Confederate authority and its implications for reconstruction. Facing overwhelming opposition, Lincoln eventually relented, admitting to navy secretary Gideon Welles that he was probably mistaken. On April 12, Lincoln asked Weitzel whether the Confederate legislature had assembled, and Weitzel responded by wiring a copy of Campbell's communication of April 7, which Lincoln had not yet seen. Any hopes Lincoln harbored for the Virginia initiative were dashed after his reading Campbell's take on it, and he ordered Weitzel to withdraw the offer.

In his communication to Weitzel, Lincoln betrayed his own misgivings. Campbell seems to have assumed, Lincoln maintained, that in originally calling for "the insurgent Legislature of Virginia" to assemble, Lincoln was recognizing it as "the rightful Legislature of the State." Lincoln countered that he had done no such thing. To the contrary, by referring in the original order to "the gentlemen who have *acted* as the Legislature of Virginia[,] in support of the rebellion," he had specifically intended to deny the legitimacy of Virginia's Confederate legislature. Moreover, his language also signaled his dealing with the legislators "as men having power *de facto* to do a specific thing"—namely, to end Virginia's support for the rebellion in return for leniency on property confiscation. "I meant this and no more," Lincoln contended. Since Campbell had misconstrued Lincoln's intentions, and, moreover, since Lee's surrender obviated the question, Lincoln put an end to the initiative.

Lincoln's language revealed both his annoyance with Campbell and a certain defensiveness, since he hardly needed to justify himself to Weitzel. Lincoln almost seemed to be trying to convince himself that the initiative had not been mistaken and that it was Campbell's misinterpretation of it that caused the problem. Campbell undoubtedly read far more into Lincoln's proposal than Lincoln had intended. And yet, as Lincoln's entire cabinet concluded without having seen Campbell's letter, the initiative contradicted Lincoln's entire approach to the Confederacy. Although Lincoln acknowledged he would never have made the offer had he known how close Lee was to surrendering, he could not admit that the plan was doomed not by poor timing but because it was a terrible idea. At one point in the episode, Lincoln half-jokingly remarked to Grant that "it seems that you are pretty effectually withdrawing the Virginia troops from opposition to the government." When it came time for Sherman, in his agreement with Johnston, to withdraw Confederate troops in North Carolina from their opposition to the government, he may well have been guilty of intruding on political questions. But his doing so was partly because Lincoln himself—in his desperation to end the war, and in his seeing the war and reconstruction as inseparable—had likewise overlooked the distinction between military and political questions.

IV

Even before the Virginia episode had ended, Lincoln delivered on the evening of April 11 his "last speech." It was hardly thought of as such at the time, and Lincoln closed the address by alluding to a forthcoming announcement on reconstruction that he never got to make. It is perhaps fitting that Lincoln's final public words, delivered at the moment of triumph, were devoted less to the war than to reconstruction, since for him the two had always been inseparable. The remarks also revealed, one final time, Lincoln's divided mind on reconstruction. The restorationist dimension was exemplified by Lincoln's repeated reference to restoring the seceded states to their "proper practical relations with the Union," while the reconstructionist dimension was symbolized by his endorsing black suffrage. However unsatisfactory Lincoln's qualified support for black voting rights may have been to some contemporaries, it was the first time in US history that a sitting president publicly endorsed black suffrage.[17]

The speech was prompted by word of Lee's surrender, which reached Washington during the evening of April 9, after Lincoln had already returned, setting off celebrations throughout the night. A crowd serenaded Lincoln at the White House the next day, but he offered only brief remarks and pledged to deliver a formal address the following day to mark the occasion. An even larger crowd amassed on the evening of April 11 to hear the promised speech. An audience expecting unapologetic triumphalism was no doubt surprised and somewhat disappointed to hear a disquisition on the Louisiana government and on reconstruction. With the recent military success, Lincoln began, "the re-inauguration of the national government—reconstruction—which has had a large share of thought from the first, is pressed much more closely upon our attention." This situation was "fraught with great difficulty," since, unlike the case in war between nations, "there is no authorized organ for us to treat with." "No one man has authority to give up the rebellion for any other man," he continued. "We simply must begin with, and mould from, disorganized and discordant elements." Neither did it help that Unionists themselves disagreed over "the mode, manner, and means of reconstruction."

The remainder of the address combined an analysis of the problem of reconstruction with a defense of Louisiana's Unionist government. Responding indirectly to criticism of that government and of his role in creating it, Lincoln outlined the story of its formation under the ten-percent plan, which, he emphasized, had received his cabinet's full support and overwhelming approval from Congress. Although Lincoln's intent was to downplay his own role in establishing and sustaining the Louisiana government, one might reasonably have concluded from his version of events that he had been intimately involved in Louisiana affairs. "From about July 1862, I had corresponded with different persons, supposed to be interested, seeking a reconstruction of a State government for Louisiana," he acknowledged, noting further his placing of Banks in charge of that task. Having promised to sustain the new Louisiana government, Lincoln added his famous Machiavellian proviso: "But, as bad promises are better broken than kept, I shall treat this as a bad promise, and break it, whenever I shall be convinced that keeping it is adverse to the public interest. But I have not yet been so convinced."

Lincoln then turned to the one issue that had plagued reconstruction from the beginning: whether the seceded states had ever left the Union. Although Lincoln's entire conception of the Confederacy and the rebellion had rested on the principle that said states had never left, he insisted that the question was "practically immaterial" and could have no other result "than the mischievous one of dividing our friends." Throughout the war, he had *purposely* forborne any public expression" on this question, which he deemed "a merely pernicious abstraction." Instead, he reasoned, invoking an imaginary consensus, "we all agree that the seceded states, so called, are out of their proper practical relation with the Union," and that the federal government's "sole object" was to restore that relation. This task would be easier without deciding, "or even considering," whether the seceded states had left. "Let us all join in doing the acts necessary to restoring the proper practical relations between these states and the Union," he advised. Only then might each person "innocently indulge his own opinion" on this question.

Just as reconstruction had always been a practical problem for Lincoln, the Louisiana government offered not a theoretical model but rather concrete progress, which, though imperfect, should not be discarded. Lincoln conceded the government's deficiencies: it was based on a mere twelve thousand loyal voters, and some critics found it unsatisfactory for failing to enact black voting rights. Lincoln then issued his famous public endorsement of black suffrage, which, though limited, was unequivocal: "I would myself prefer that it were now conferred on the very intelligent, and on those who serve our cause as soldiers." These shortcomings notwithstanding, the issue was not whether Louisiana's government was perfect, but whether the state's restoration could be better achieved by working with or by repudiating it. "Can Louisiana be brought into proper practical relation with the Union," he asked rhetorically, "*sooner* by *sustaining*, or by *discarding* her new State government?"

From here, Lincoln delineated the progress of Louisiana's reconstruction. Twelve thousand citizens had abandoned the Confederacy and resumed their Union allegiance; had held elections and created a new government that had ratified the Thirteenth Amendment; and had written a constitution abolishing slavery, providing for public education "equally to black and white," and authorizing the state legislature to adopt black suffrage. These twelve thousand persons were thus committed to the Union and to "perpetual freedom," and, having done all that was asked of them, they sought recognition and assistance. "Now, if we reject, and spurn them," Lincoln warned, "we do our utmost to disorganize and disperse them." Repudiating the Louisiana government would demoralize white Unionists and former slaves, and it could not possibly help the state's restoration, whereas recognizing and sustaining the government would have the opposite effect. White Unionists would be encouraged to "adhere to their work" and strive for "a complete success," while "the colored man too, in seeing all united for him," would be similarly "inspired with vigilance, and energy, and daring, to the same end." To be sure, black men desired the right to vote, but would not this goal be more readily attained, Lincoln asked, "by saving the already advanced steps toward it, than by running backward over them?" He then employed his incongruous "fowl-egg" metaphor, which his critics greatly derided. "Concede that the new government of Louisiana is only to what it should be as the egg is to the fowl, we shall sooner have the fowl by hatching the egg than by smashing it?" He ended this discussion with the familiar refrain: "Can Louisiana be brought into proper practical relation with the Union *sooner* by *sustaining* or by *discarding* her new State Government?"

Lincoln concluded by pledging that while almost everything he said about Louisiana applied to the other seceded states, "no exclusive, and inflexible plan" would be unilaterally imposed on all of them. Yet he added: "Important principles may, and must, be inflexible." He then observed that "some new announcement to the people of the South" would likely be forthcoming, but these were the last words Abraham Lincoln addressed to the American people.

Although Lincoln's speech captured both the continuities and dis-continuities of his approach to reconstruction, observers have tended to emphasize the former, citing the speech to highlight Lincoln's es-sential conservatism. To be sure, by explicitly defining reconstruction as "the re-inauguration of the national government," which had been going on "from the first," Lincoln clearly evinced his restorationist mindset. He overwhelmingly focused on the goal of restoring the se-ceded states to their "proper practical relations" with the Union, and in doing so he defended a Louisiana government about which many contemporaries had serious doubts. Meanwhile, Lincoln effectively appeared to ignore questions pertaining to the deeper social and economic reordering of southern society, and even his endorsement of limited black suffrage can be seen as an overture to the Radical Republicans and thus as an example of his pragmatism.

And yet, the speech also reflected how far Lincoln had come in so short a time. As late as fall 1862, Lincoln conceived of a post-emancipation United States as one without black people, who were in but not of American society and thus would best be resettled elsewhere. Now, no sooner had hostilities effectively ended than he publically endorsed black suffrage. The same Lincoln who had so carefully calibrated his policies on slavery and race to northern public opinion was now taking a position—on one of the most volatile issues of the day—far in advance of public sentiment. Indeed, by simply mentioning that black men desired the right to vote, Lincoln was publicly acknowledging that their views were a legitimate part of the political equation—something no sitting president had ever done.

Moreover, while Lincoln did not substantively address social or economic issues, his speech reflected a growing solicitude for black freedom. He applauded Louisiana's new constitution for *not* adopting apprenticeship, which he had formerly endorsed, and for authorizing black education as well as black voting rights. And in defending the Louisiana government, Lincoln warned that by rejecting it, the nation would be saying to the former slaves: "This cup of liberty which these, your old masters, hold to your lips, we will dash from you, and leave you to the chances of gathering the spilled and scattered contents in some vague and undefined when, where, and how." Lincoln's view of the South's "old masters"—who would voluntarily hold the "cup of liberty" to the lips of their former slaves—may have been unrealistic. But he also affirmed that the former slaves' enjoyment of the "cup of liberty" must not be postponed to an indeterminate future, to "some vague and undefined when, where, and how."

Rather than his conservativism, Lincoln's last speech perhaps better illustrates the unresolved tensions between his two modes of thought on reconstruction. Although Lincoln had come to define reconstruction more broadly, he did not quite seem to realize that the restorationist and reconstructionist dimensions of his thinking were ultimately incompatible. The seceded states could hardly be restored to their "proper practical relations" with the Union so long as the implications of the abolition of slavery remained unsettled. The very idea of "practical" relations was almost logically absurd until that issue had been resolved. In essence, this is what Lincoln's radical critics had been saying all along. As has often been noted, one audience member thought he understood the implications of Lincoln's remarks. "That means nigger citizenship," murmured John Wilkes Booth. "That is the last speech he will ever make." When one of his coconspirators refused to shoot Lincoln right then and there, Booth vowed: "By God, I'll put him through."

Lincoln no more considered this speech his last than he did his cabinet meeting of that fateful April 14. Whereas this meeting marks Lincoln's final words on reconstruction for the historical record, at the time it was merely a first step toward addressing the postwar situation. With Seward's son and secretary, Frederick, sitting in for the injured Seward, and with Grant in attendance, the cabinet discussed the issue of maintaining order in the seceded states until loyal governments could be established. Having abandoned his idea of working with the Confederate legislatures, Lincoln remained adamant, according to navy secretary Welles, that the federal government not control this process. "Their people must do that," Lincoln insisted, "though I reckon that at first some of them may do it badly."

Stanton then presented a plan drawn up at Lincoln's request but which Lincoln had only seen the previous day. It called for appointing military governors for the seceded states until civilian governments could be created, and for military authorities to provide law and order while federal executive departments reestablished operations. Lincoln approved the plan, which, he observed, substantively resembled one the cabinet had previously discussed. One problem, however, was that it provided for a single military governor for both Virginia and North Carolina, prompting objections that it contradicted the principle of state individuality, which Lincoln had just endorsed in his recent speech, and called into question Virginia's existing government. Lincoln asked Stanton to revise the plan to account for the two states' different circumstances. "We must not," he noted, "stultify ourselves as regards Virginia, but we must help her." The cabinet agreed that North Carolina, once order had been restored and a loyal government created, might provide a model for the other states. Lincoln asked Stanton to have the revised plan ready for the following week's cabinet meeting, and he invited his advisers to give careful consideration to the question of reconstruction, since "no greater or more important one could come before us, or any future Cabinet."

Lincoln observed that it was providential that the war had ended while Congress was not in session, thus allowing the administration a free hand on reconstruction. "If we were wise and discreet," he remarked, "we should reanimate the States and get their governments in successful operations, with order prevailing and the Union reestablished before Congress came together in December." There were some in Congress, he continued, "who, if their motives were good, were nevertheless impracticable, and who possessed feelings of hate and vindictiveness in which he did not sympathize and could not participate." Referring to congressional criticism of the Louisiana government, he lamented the desire of "some of our very good friends" to dictate terms to the defeated states and "to treat the people not as fellow citizens." He reiterated his wish that Louisiana had implemented black suffrage, but he maintained that the matter of voting rights was best left to the states and gave no indication that he would require black suffrage as a term of readmission. Talk then turned to military matters, with Grant providing an account of Lee's surrender and offering assurance of Johnston's impending surrender. Although Lincoln indicated no major alteration of his reconstruction policy at his last cabinet meeting, Stanton's plan, which continued the wartime practice of providing military governors for the seceded states, was less a substantive program of postwar reconstruction than a means of establishing the order essential to one. Despite Lincoln's talk about the people of the seceded states taking the lead in reconstruction, Stanton's proposal clearly suggested that loyal governments would be created under close federal oversight.[18]

Lincoln later conferred with Vice President Andrew Johnson, who had not attended the meeting and with whom Lincoln had not met since the inauguration. No record of their talk survives, but they no doubt discussed reconstruction matters, including the progress of Tennessee's government. By the next day, Andrew Johnson was president.

EPILOGUE
What If

One of American history's great "what-ifs" involves the question of how postwar reconstruction—and much that followed from it, including the tortured history of race relations—might have been different had Lincoln not been struck down by an assassin's bullet. Although speculation is not ordinarily the historian's task, scholars have examined Lincoln's wartime reconstruction measures in order to hypothesize on what he might have done after the war. Because postwar reconstruction was so disastrous under Andrew Johnson, speculation on how Lincoln might have guided the nation through this period has had a decidedly firm hold on the American imagination.

Given how integral the consequences of emancipation were to postwar reconstruction, how central race relations have been to American history, and how large Lincoln looms in the nation's psyche, it is understandable that Lincoln's views on race and their implications for reconstruction have attracted so much attention. Scholars have focused in particular on whether Lincoln would have supported legal and political equality as essential components of postwar reconstruction. In doing so, some have noted the paradox that it was Johnson's very racism and intransigence—in restoring southern antebellum and former Confederate leaders to power and refusing to adjust his policy when they denied black people basic civil rights—that compelled Republicans to adopt equality before the law and black suffrage. The implication is that a more moderately tempered and presumably more conservative Lincoln would not have provoked the political crisis that eventuated in "Radical Reconstruction," the Fourteenth and Fifteenth Amendments to the US Constitution, and a host of other measures that spawned decades of southern white resentment.

This line of reasoning has some merit. However, the various issues that resulted from Confederate defeat and the abolition of slavery—defining black civil rights; determining representation in Congress with elimination of the "three-fifths" clause; imposing political proscriptions on former Confederate leaders; invalidating the Confederate debt and guaranteeing the federal one; prohibiting compensation to former slaveholders for the loss of their slave property; and, ultimately, guaranteeing black voting rights—would have been unavoidable even under Lincoln. These issues probably would have caused some conflict between Lincoln and congressional Republicans (and Congress in general), but the dictates of party and nation would have compelled them to find a workable solution. Moreover, taking into account the evolution of Lincoln's racial views over the course of the war, it does not require a particularly bold leap of historical imagination to envision Lincoln requiring—as a condition of the postwar settlement—a program of equality before the law and black suffrage very similar to the one Republicans eventually implemented in place of Johnson's policy and in response to white southern resistance. Lincoln's racial views thus remain central to an alternative history of postwar reconstruction or of American race relations.

Hypothetically, had Lincoln and congressional Republicans been able to craft a program of equality before the law and universal (not limited) black suffrage, backed by the full power of the federal government and presented to the former Confederate states soon after the end of the war as a fundamental condition of readmission, the course of American history might have been very different. As the experience of Radical Reconstruction would show, such a program would have had broad ramifications for remaking southern society, extending not only to voting and office holding but also to the shaping and implementing of the law and public policy in myriad ways affecting everyday life. In short, substantive black access to political power and to the mechanisms of the state would have profoundly altered the course of postwar reconstruction. Initiated at the time of Confederate defeat by a president and Congress working in unison—instead of two years later by a president and Congress at loggerheads—such a program might have had a chance of success. Assessing how Lincoln would have responded to continued southern white resistance and violence moves yet further into the realm of speculation, but the historical record shows that he would not have remained wedded to a policy that did not work.

Pondering history's what-ifs can be fruitful, and speculation on these matters marks the intersecting of Americans' obsession with race and their infatuation with Lincoln. Even though generations of Americans have fixated on the implications of Lincoln's racial views for the nation's history, the limits of Lincoln's approach to reconstruction would not necessarily have been reached on the question of black legal and political equality. Instead, they would have been reached on what might be thought of as matters of political economy—including labor and relations between former slaveholders and former slaves, land, and property rights. From what we know of Lincoln's views on these matters—even allowing for the possibility of those views evolving, and for meaningful black political power—it becomes much more difficult to envision him embracing the kinds of policies that a fundamental transformation of plantation society and the southern social order would have required. This is not to suggest that historians have overstated the importance of Lincoln's racial thought and its implications for postwar reconstruction, but rather that their traditional focus on them has perhaps been somewhat misplaced.

Hailing from famously humble origins, Lincoln personified the openness and upward social mobility of northern society, and he symbolized the world of those small property holders and independent producers who constituted the backbone of the Republican Party before the Civil War. Lincoln's understanding of labor and labor relations was rooted in the northern free-labor ideology, which assumed a harmony of interests between capital and labor in allowing wage workers and other dependent laborers to rise to the status of independent property holder. The notion of free labor having an inherently exploitative quality, or of capital and labor being locked in immutable class struggle, was entirely foreign to Lincoln. For him, it was slavery that constituted systematic economic robbery and class warfare.

The free-labor outlook formed the basis of Lincoln's critique of southern slave society, but its applicability to the postemancipation South would have presented him with almost insurmountable difficulties. Following the Emancipation Proclamation and wartime free-labor initiatives in the Union-occupied South, Lincoln at least began to reevaluate his views on southern labor and to think seriously about the challenges of reconstituting relations between former masters and former slaves. As the historical record would eventually show, the problem of applying the free-labor vision to a plantation society, especially given slavery's bitter racial legacy, proved to be virtually impossible. Lincoln undoubtedly would have overseen the mandate of the Freedmen's Bureau to provide humanitarian aid, relieve suffering and dislocation, and establish schools and court systems, as well as to implement free labor in the postwar South. And he can be credited with having begun to conceptualize the problem of reorganizing the South's labor system. However, given his northern free-labor outlook, Lincoln, had he lived, would not have been able to solve a problem that probably defied solution.

Whereas Lincoln may have begun to think about the problem of labor in the postwar South, the same cannot be said of his approach to land, or to black aspirations for property as the means to economic independence. By the end of his life, Lincoln had hardly turned his attention in any serious or systematic way to the problem of property inequality in southern society, or to the challenges such inequality would have presented to black freedom, especially in light of the importance of property to nineteenth-century conceptions of freedom and independence. For a host of reasons, systematic land confiscation in the postwar South did not happen. If anything, it would have been even less likely under Lincoln. Indeed, given his essentially moderate temperament, aversion to radical measures, and commitment to the sanctity of bourgeois property rights grounded in a system of law, it is virtually impossible to conceive of Lincoln supporting any policy designed to break the power of the South's planter elite, which would have been an essential first step to genuine social and economic reconstruction.

Ultimately, Lincoln could not have addressed any of these issues without first coming to terms with the tensions between the restorationist and reconstructionist dimensions of his approach to reconstruction. During the war, the latter had not so much replaced as supplemented the former. Lincoln never abandoned his restorationist approach, but he came to realize that reconstruction would involve more than simply restoring the seceded states to their "proper practical relations with the Union"; it would also have to include grappling with the consequences of emancipation. And yet, the historical record offers no evidence that Lincoln ever recognized the incompatibility of the two approaches, and he likely would have retained elements of his restorationist mindset well into the postwar period. Tragically for the nation, Andrew Johnson and others like him were convinced that restoration was all Lincoln had ever had in mind, and that their policies were just an extension of his. But this was not the case. How far Lincoln thinking's on reconstruction would have evolved, as he confronted the challenges of the postwar world, remains among American history's what-ifs.

NOTES
BIBLIOGRAPHY
INDEX

NOTES

Introduction

1. Du Bois, *Writings*, 1196. See also: Fredrickson, *Big Enough to Be Inconsistent*.
2. This section reflects my own reading of Lincoln on slavery and race, but it also benefits from Foner, *The Fiery Trial*, chaps. 1–4.
3. Lincoln, "Speech at Chicago, Illinois," July 10, 1858; "Speech at Peoria, Illinois," October 16, 1854, *Collected Works*, 2:247–83 (1854 speech), 484–502 (1858 speech).
4. Lincoln, "Seventh and Last Debate with Stephen A. Douglas at Alton, Illinois," October 15, 1858, *Collected Works*, 3:283–325.
5. Oakes, *The Radical and the Republican*, 119–31. See also: Oakes, "Natural Rights, Citizenship Rights, States' Rights, and Black Rights: Another Look at Lincoln and Race," in Foner, *Our Lincoln*, 109–134.
6. Burlingame and Ettlinger, eds., *Inside Lincoln's White House*, 69 (July 31, 1863).

1. From Restoration to Emancipation (March 1861–January 1863)

1. Holzer, Lincoln, *President-Elect*, chaps. 9–11.
2. Lincoln, "First Inaugural Address—Final Text," March 4, 1861, *Collected Works*, 4:262–71.
3. Lincoln, "Message to Congress in Special Session," July 4, 1861, *Collected Works*, 4:421–41.
4. Lincoln, "Proclamation Calling Militia and Convening Congress," April 15, 1861, *Collected Works*, 4:331–32.
5. Belz, *Reconstructing the Union*, 8–13.
6. Lincoln, "Message to Congress in Special Session," July 4, 1861, *Collected Works*, 4:421–41.
7. Harris, *With Charity for All*, 20–23.
8. McPherson has made this point most definitively in *Tried by War*.
9. Lincoln, "Message to Congress in Special Session," July 4, 1861, *Collected Works*, 4:421–41.
10. Siddali, *From Property to Person*, 253–54.
11. Lincoln to Orville H. Browning, September 22, 1861, *Collected Works*, 4:531–33.
12. Foner, "Lincoln and Colonization," in Foner, *Our Lincoln*.
13. Lincoln, "Annual Message to Congress," December 3, 1861, *Collected Works*, 5:35–53.

14. Lincoln, "Message to Congress," March 6, 1862, *Collected Works*, 5:144–46.
15. Donald, *Lincoln*, 342–48.
16. Grimsley, *The Hard Hand of War*.
17. Harris, *With Charity for All*, chaps. 2–4, on the appointment of military governors and political affairs in general in Union-occupied areas in 1861 and 1862; Lincoln to Andrew Johnson, July 3, 1862, *Collected Works*, 5:302–3.
18. Lincoln, "Proclamation Revoking General Hunter's Order of Military Emancipation," May 19, 1862, *Collected Works*, 5:222–24.
19. Lincoln, "Appeal to Border State Representatives to Favor Compensated Emancipation," July 12, 1862, *Collected Works*, 5:317–19.
20. Siddali, *From Property to Person*, 257–61; Lincoln, "To the Senate and House of Representatives," *Collected Works*, 5:328–31.
21. Lincoln, "Address on Colonization to a Deputation of Negroes," August 14, 1862; Lincoln to Horace Greeley, August 22, 1862, *Collected Works*, 5:370–75, 388–89.
22. Lincoln, "Preliminary Emancipation Proclamation," September 22, 1862, *Collected Works*, 5:433–36.
23. Lincoln to George F. Shepley, November 21, 1862, *Collected Works*, 5:504–5; Belz, *Reconstructing the Union*, 66–110.
24. Lincoln, "Annual Message to Congress," December 1, 1862, *Collected Works*, 5:518–37.
25. Lincoln, "Emancipation Proclamation," January 1, 1863, *Collected Works*, 6:28–31.
26. Foner, *Forever Free*, 51.
27. This argument is made most cogently in Harris, *With Charity for All*.

2. From Emancipation to Reconstruction
(January–December 1863)

1. Belz, *Reconstructing the Union*, 110–15.
2. Belz, *Reconstructing the Union*, 116–25, 126–43.
3. Harris, *With Charity for All*, 100–105; Belz, *Reconstructing the Union*, 116.
4. Lincoln, "Opinion on the Admission of West Virginia into the Union," [December 31, 1862], *Collected Works*, 6:26–28 (emphasis in original); Belz, *Reconstructing the Union*, 116.
5. Harris, *With Charity for All*, 105–12.
6. Harris, *With Charity for All*, 112–17; Belz, *Reconstructing the Union*, 143–45; Taylor, *Louisiana Reconstructed*, 2–24.
7. Lincoln to E. E. Malhiot, Bradish Johnson, and Thomas Cottman, June 19, 1863; Lincoln, "Memorandum," [June 19, 1863], *Collected Works*, 6:287–89.

8. Donald, *Lincoln*, 412–21.

9. Lincoln, "Message to Congress in Special Session," July 4, 1861, *Collected Works*, 4:421–41.

10. Lincoln to the Workingmen of Manchester, England, January 19, 1863, *Collected Works*, 6:63–65. See also: Lincoln to the Workingmen of London, February 2, 1863; Lincoln, "Resolution on Slavery," April 15, 1863, *Collected Works*, 6:88–89, 176–77. This section also makes considerable use of Foner, *The Fiery Trial*, chap. 8.

11. Lincoln to Andrew Johnson, March 26, 1863, *Collected Works*, 6:149–50. See also: Lincoln to John A. McClernand, January 8, 1863; Lincoln to John A. Dix, January 14, 1863; Lincoln to David Hunter, April 1, 1863, *Collected Works*, 6:48–49, 56, 158.

12. Lincoln, "Response to a Serenade," July 7, 1863, *Collected Works*, 6:319–20.

13. Lincoln, "Endorsement on Letter of James R. Gilmore to Zebulon B. Vance, [July 15? 1863], *Collected Works*, 6:330–31.

14. Lincoln to James C. Conkling, August 26, 1863, *Collected Works*, 6:406–10. See also, Lincoln, "Fragment," [c. August 26, 1863?]; Lincoln to James C. Conkling, August 31, 1863, *Collected Works*, 6:410–11, 423.

15. Lincoln, "Address Delivered at the Dedication of the Cemetery at Gettysburg," November 19, 1863, *Collected Works*, 7:17–23; Donald, *Lincoln*, 459–66.

16. Lincoln to Andrew Johnson, September 11, 1863, *Collected Works*, 6:440–41; Harris, *With Charity for All*, 105–12.

17. Lincoln to Stephen A. Hurlbut, July 31, 1863, *Collected Works*, 6:358–59; Harris, *With Charity for All*, 83–86.

18. Lincoln to John M. Schofield, June 22, 1863; Lincoln to Stephen A. Hurlbut, July 31, 1863, *Collected Works*, 6:291, 358–59.

19. This discussion of Louisiana affairs relies on Harris, *With Charity for All*, 117–20 (quotation p. 118), Belz, *Reconstructing the Union*, 143–52; and Cox, *Lincoln and Black Freedom*, chap. 2.

20. Lincoln to Nathaniel P. Banks, August 5, 1863, *Collected Works*, 6:364–66.

21. Lincoln to Nathaniel P. Banks, November 5, 1863, *Collected Works*, 7:1–2.

22. Banks to Lincoln, December 6, 1863, *Collected Works*, 7:90–91n.

23. Lincoln to Nathaniel P. Banks, December 24, 1863, *Collected Works*, 7:89–91. See also: Lincoln, "Memorandum Concerning Louisiana Affairs," December 16, 1863; Lincoln to Nathaniel P. Banks, December 29, 1863, *Collected Works*, 7:71, 95–96.

24. Lincoln, "Annual Message to Congress," December 8, 1863; "Proclamation of Amnesty and Reconstruction," December 8, 1863, *Collected Works*, 7:36–53 (especially pp. 48–53), 53–56. This discussion also relies on Harris, *With Charity for All*, chap. 6; Belz, *Reconstructing the Union*, 153–67; Donald, *Lincoln*, 467–74; Foner, *Reconstruction*, 35–37; and Vorenberg, *Final Freedom*, 46–48.

3. War, Reconstruction, and Reelection (December 1863–November 1864)

1. Harris, *With Charity for All*, 143–47, 149–58.

2. Harris, *With Charity for All*, 161–70.

3. Harris, *With Charity for All*, 212–17.

4. Harris, *With Charity for All*, 197–209.

5. This discussion of Louisiana affairs follows Harris, *With Charity for All*, 172–85; Taylor, *Louisiana Reconstructed*, 21–32, 41–52; and Cox, *Lincoln and Black Freedom*, chaps. 2–3.

6. Lincoln to Michael Hahn, March 13, 1864, *Collected Works*, 7:243.

7. There is a significant literature on the Wade-Davis controversy. Virtually every general history of reconstruction deals with it, and it figures prominently in the scholarship on Lincoln and reconstruction. The account presented here relies on Belz, *Reconstructing the Union*, chaps. 7–8; Harris, *With Charity for All*, 186–90; Donald, *Lincoln*, 510–12; Vorenberg, *Final Freedom*, 142–46; and Foner, *Forever Free*, 60–62.

8. Lincoln to Edwin M. Stanton, February 5, 1864, *Collected Works*, 7:169–70.

9. Lincoln, "Proclamation Concerning Reconstruction," July 8, 1864, *Collected Works*, 7:433–34.

10. Hyman, ed., *The Radical Republicans and Reconstruction*, doc. no. 16.

11. Lincoln to Horace Greeley, July 9, 1864, *Collected Works*, 7:435–36. See Lincoln's further correspondence with Greeley and John Hay, *Collected Works*, 7:440–43.

12. Lincoln, "To Whom It May Concern," July 18, 1864, *Collected Works*, 7:451. See also: Lincoln, "Memorandum on Clement C. Clay," [c. July 25], 1864; and Lincoln to Abram Wakeman, July 25, 1864, *Collected Works*, 7:459–61.

13. Lincoln to Charles D. Robinson, August 17, 1864, *Collected Works*, 7:499–502, including Robinson's letter to Lincoln.

14. Lincoln, "Interview with Alexander W. Randall and Joseph T. Mills," August 19, 1864, *Collected Works*, 7:506–508; Foner, ed., *Life and Writings of Frederick Douglass*, 3:423.

15. Lincoln to Henry J. Raymond, August 24, 1864, *Collected Works*, 7:517–18, including Raymond's letter to Lincoln and Nicolay's account of the meeting; Lincoln, "Memorandum Concerning His Probable Failure of Re-election," August 23, 1864, *Collected Works*, 7:514–15.

16. Lincoln to Isaac M. Schermerhorn, September 12, 1864, *Collected Works*, 8:1–2.

17. Oakes, *The Radical and the Republican*, 229–37. While this section presents my own summary of Lincoln's views, it has also benefitted from Oakes's work, Foner, *The Fiery Trial*, chaps. 8–9, and Fredrickson, *Big Enough to Be Inconsistent*, chap. 3.

18. Burlingame, *Abraham Lincoln*, chap. 9.

19. Lincoln, "Address at Sanitary Fair, Baltimore, Maryland," April 18, 1864, *Collected Works*, 7:301–303; Foner, *The Fiery Trial*, 276.

20. Harris, *With Charity for All*, 158–60.

21. Harris, *With Charity for All*, 209–10.

22. Lincoln to Stephen A. Hurlbut, November 14, 1864; and Lincoln to E. R. S. Canby, December 12, 1864, *Collected Works*, 8:106–08, 163–65; Harris, *With Charity for All*, 190–96; Taylor, *Louisiana Reconstructed*, 53–58.

23. Lincoln to William B. Campbell and Others, October 22, 1864, *Collected Works*, 8:58–72; Harris, *With Charity for All*, 217–23.

4. "Into Proper Practical Relations with the Union" (November 1864–April 1865)

1. Donald, *Lincoln*, 550–52; Belz, *Reconstructing the Union*, 244–48.

2. Lincoln, "Annual Message to Congress," December 6, 1864, *Collected Works*, 8:136–53; Harris, *With Charity for All*, 231–33.

3. Lincoln, "Response to a Serenade," February 1, 1865, *Collected Works*, 8:254–55; Vorenberg, *Final Freedom*, chap. 7; Foner, *The Fiery Trial*, 311–14.

4. This discussion of the Hampton Roads conference is based on documents in *Collected Works*, 8:220–21, 243, 246–48, 250–52, 256, 258, 260–61, and 274–87; and on Donald, *Lincoln*, 555–61; Foner, *The Fiery Trial*, 314–16; Harris, *With Charity for All*, 238–39, and Escott, *"What Shall We Do with the Negro?"* chap. 7.

5. Belz, *Reconstructing the Union*, 250–67; Harris, *With Charity for All*, 233–38; and Cox, *Lincoln and Black Freedom*, 119–21.

6. Burlingame and Ettlinger, eds., *Inside Lincoln's White House*, 253 (December 18, 1864).

7. Harris, *With Charity for All*, 210–11.

8. Harris, *With Charity for All*, 223–27.

9. Harris, *With Charity for All*, 246–47; Foner, *The Fiery Trial*, 318; Taylor, *Louisiana Reconstructed*, 53–58; and Cox, *Lincoln and Black Freedom*, chap. 4.

10. Harris, *With Charity for All*, 244–46; Belz, *Reconstructing the Union*, 267–76; and Donald, *Lincoln*, 561–65.

11. McKitrick, "Party Politics and the Union and Confederate War Efforts."

12. Quoted in Oakes, *The Radical and the Republican*, 168.

13. Lincoln, "Second Inaugural Address," March 4, 1865, *Collected Works*, 8:332–33; Foner, *The Fiery Trial*, 323–28.

14. Lincoln to Ulysses S. Grant, March 3, 1865, *Collected Works*, 8:331–32.

15. Sherman, *Memoirs*, 813. On the City Point meeting and the Sherman-Johnston surrender: Donald, *Lincoln*, 573–74; Harris, *With Charity for All*, 248–50; Marszalek, *Sherman*, 337–38, 341–46.

16. This discussion of Lincoln's Virginia initiative is based on documents in *Collected Works*, 8:386–89, 405–408; and on Donald, *Lincoln*, 576–80, 589–90; Harris, *With Charity for All*, 250–53; and Belz, *Reconstructing the Union*, 279–81.

17. Lincoln, "Last Public Address," April 11, 1865, *Collected Works*, 8:399–405. On the circumstances surrounding the address and on its contents: Donald, *Lincoln*, 580–85; Harris, *With Charity for All*, 255–58; and Foner, *The Fiery Trial*, 330–32.

18. Donald, *Lincoln*, 590–92; Harris, *With Charity for All*, 263–64; and Foner, *The Fiery Trial*, 332.

BIBLIOGRAPHY

This bibliography is limited to works actually cited and to other studies that deal substantively with Lincoln and Reconstruction, some of which have been consulted but not cited. It makes no attempt to include the extensive literature on those other aspects of Lincoln's life and career and on the Civil War era that figure in this study.

Belz, Herman. *Reconstructing the Union: Theory and Policy during the Civil War*. Ithaca, NY: Cornell University Press, 1969.

Burlingame, Michael. *Abraham Lincoln: A Life*. 2 vols. Baltimore: Johns Hopkins University Press, 2008.

Burlingame, Michael, and John R. Turner Ettlinger, eds. *Inside Lincoln's White House: The Complete Civil War Diary of John Hay*. Carbondale: Southern Illinois University Press, 1997.

Cox, LaWanda. *Lincoln and Black Freedom: A Study in Presidential Leadership*. Columbia: University of South Carolina Press, 1981.

Donald, David Herbert. *Lincoln*. New York: Simon and Schuster, 1995.

Du Bois, W. E. B. *Writings*. New York: Library of America, 1986.

Escott, Paul D. *"What Shall We Do with the Negro?" Lincoln, White Racism, and Civil War America*. Charlottesville: University of Virginia Press, 2009.

Foner, Eric. *The Fiery Trial: Abraham Lincoln and American Slavery*. New York: W. W. Norton, 2010.

———. *Forever Free: The Story of Emancipation and Reconstruction*. New York: Vintage, 2005.

———. *Reconstruction: America's Unfinished Revolution, 1863–1877*. New York: Harper and Row, 1988.

———, ed. *Our Lincoln: New Perspectives on Lincoln and His World*. New York: W. W. Norton, 2008.

Foner, Philip S., ed. *The Life and Writings of Frederick Douglass*. 5 vols. New York: International, 1950–1955, 1975.

Fredrickson, George M. *Big Enough to Be Inconsistent: Abraham Lincoln Confronts Slavery and Race*. Cambridge, MA: Harvard University Press, 2008.

Grimsley, Mark. *The Hard Hand of War: Union Military Policy toward Southern Civilians, 1861–1865*. Cambridge, UK: Cambridge University Press, 1995.

Harris, William C. *With Charity for All: Lincoln and the Restoration of the Union*. Lexington: University of Kentucky Press, 1997.

Hesseltine, William B. *Lincoln's Plan of Reconstruction*. Tuscaloosa, AL: Confederate Publishing Co., 1960.

Holt, Michael F. "Abraham Lincoln and the Politics of Union." In *Abraham Lincoln and the American Political Tradition*, edited by John L. Thomas, 111–41. Amherst: University of Massachusetts Press, 1986.

Holzer, Harold. *Lincoln President-Elect: Abraham Lincoln and the Great Secession Winter, 1860–1861*. New York: Simon and Schuster, 2008.

Hyman, Harold M., ed. *The Radical Republicans and Reconstruction*. Indianapolis: Bobbs-Merrill, 1967.

Johnson, Michael P., ed. *Abraham Lincoln, Slavery, and the Civil War: Selected Writings and Speeches*. 2nd ed. Boston: Bedford/St. Martin's, 2011.

Lincoln, Abraham. *The Collected Works of Abraham Lincoln*. Edited by Roy P. Basler. 9 vols. New Brunswick, NJ: Rutgers University Press, 1953–1955.

Marszalek, John F. *Sherman: A Soldier's Passion for Order*. New York: Free Press, 1993.

McCrary, Peyton. *Abraham Lincoln and Reconstruction: The Louisiana Experiment*. Princeton, NJ: Princeton University Press, 1978.

McKitrick, Eric. "Party Politics and the Union and Confederate War Efforts." In *The American Party Systems: Stages of Political Development*, edited by William Nisbet Chambers and Walter Dean Burnham, 117–51. New York: Oxford University Press, 1967.

McPherson, James M. *Tried by War: Abraham Lincoln as Commander in Chief*. New York: Penguin, 2008.

Oakes, James. *The Radical and the Republican: Frederick Douglass, Abraham Lincoln, and the Triumph of Antislavery Politics*. New York: W. W. Norton, 2007.

Sherman, William Tecumseh. *Memoirs of General W. T. Sherman*. New York: Library of America, 1990.

Siddali, Silvana R. *From Property to Person: Slavery and the Confiscation Acts, 1861–1862*. Baton Rouge: Louisiana State University Press, 2005.

Simpson, Brooks D. *The Reconstruction Presidents*. Lawrence: University Press of Kansas, 1998.

Taylor, Joe Gray. *Louisiana Reconstructed, 1863–1877*. Baton Rouge: Louisiana State University Press, 1974.

Tunnell, Ted. *Crucible of Reconstruction: War, Radicalism and Race in Louisiana, 1862–1877*. Baton Rouge: Louisiana State University Press, 1984.

Vorenberg, Michael. *Final Freedom: The Civil War, the Abolition of Slavery, and the Thirteenth Amendment*. Cambridge, UK: Cambridge University Press, 2001.

Williams, T. Harry. *Lincoln and the Radicals*. Madison: University of Wisconsin Press, 1960.

INDEX

abolitionists, 7, 22, 30, 103

African Americans: and Lincoln, 5, 7–12, 24–26, 38, 42–43, 54–61, 63–65, 67–70, 81–82, 96–103, 111, 136–41, 143–47; and military service, 42, 56–57, 59, 98, 124. *See also* black suffrage; race

Alabama, 77, 104

Antietam (battle), 34

apprenticeship, 69–70, 100, 140

Arkansas, 20–21, 61–62, 78–79, 88, 104–5, 122, 125

Army of the Potomac, 46

Ashley, James, 117, 121: and reconstruction bill, 121–23, 125

Attorney General. *See* Bates, Edward

Banks, Nathaniel P., 51–52, 63–66, 79–81, 105–6, 121, 124, 137

Bates, Edward, and ruling on black citizenship, 41, 84, 97, 121

Belz, Herman, 19, 50, 85

black suffrage, 73, 80, 144: and Lincoln, 5, 10, 71, 81–82, 98, 111, 121–22, 136–47; and Wade-Davis bill, 84–86. *See also* African Americans; race

Blair, Francis, Sr., 116–17

Booth, John Wilkes, 141

border states, 16, 21–24, 26–28, 30–32, 37, 40, 62, 70–71, 106, 115, 119

Brownlow, William G., 123

Buell, Don Carlos, 28, 46

Bull Run (first battle of), 22

Bureau of Refugees, Freedmen, and Abandoned Lands, 126, 146

Burlingame, Michael, 99

Burnside, Ambrose E., 46

Butler, Benjamin F., 23, 51, 77–78

Campbell, John A., 117, 131–36

Canby, E. R. S., 104–6

Chancellorsville (battle), 46

Charles I, 118

Chase, Salmon P., 81, 84, 103, 112

Chickamauga (battle), 61

City Point (Virginia), 129–30

Civil War: and Lincoln, 2, 5–6, 12–13, 129–31; military aspects of, 22, 26–28, 34, 44–6, 50, 56–57, 61, 66, 76, 78, 81, 83, 89, 103–5, 111, 122–23, 129–31. *See also* Confederate States of America; reconstruction; secession

colonization, 11, 24–27, 34, 37–40, 97

compensated emancipation, and Lincoln, 26–27, 30–32, 34–35, 37–41, 97, 119–20

Confederate States of America: and Lincoln, 2–3, 12–22, 26, 35–38, 42–43, 48–49, 72–74, 86, 109–10, 113–18, 125, 128, 131–35, 137–38; negotiations with, 6, 18–19, 44–46, 54, 57–58, 60, 89–96, 107, 110, 116–20; and Radical Republicans, 19–20. *See also* Civil War; reconstruction; secession

confiscation (land), 5, 101–3, 126, 132, 146–47

confiscation acts: first (1861), 23, 26; second (1862), 33, 35

Congress, 17, 23, 27, 32–33, 35, 40, 49, 81, 104–5, 108, 115, 144–45: and reconstruction policy, 29, 36–37, 47, 83–89, 112–13, 120–22, 125–27, 142. *See also* Congressional Republicans; Radical Republicans

Congressional Republicans, 4, 6, 21, 26, 81: and reconstruction policy, 47, 75–76, 83–89, 125–27, 144–45. *See also* Congress; Radical Republicans

Conkling, James C., 58; Lincoln's public letter to, 58–60

Conservative Unionists (Louisiana), 52–53, 63–64

contrabands (fugitive slaves), 23

Davis, Henry Winter, 83
Davis, Jefferson, 90, 93–95, 113, 116
Declaration of Independence, 10, 60
Delaware, 22, 26
Democrats (northern), 22, 53–54, 57, 76–77, 91–95, 103–6, 115, 117, 125, 127
Direct Tax Act (1862), 102
Douglas, Stephen A., 10
Douglass, Frederick, 13, 93–97, 99
Dred Scott decision, 10, 41
Du Bois, W. E. B., 4
Durant, Thomas J., 80–81, 105

Early, Jubal, 83–84
Emancipation Proclamation, 3, 15, 22–23, 26, 37, 44, 96–97, 133, 146: exemptions from, 37, 42, 47, 51–52; final version of, 42–43; Lincoln's decision to issue, 28–34; Lincoln's defense of, 45, 53–61, 89–96, 98, 114, 118–19; preliminary version of, 34–37, 49

Fifteenth Amendment, 144
Fishback, William M., 79, 122
Flanders, Benjamin F., 36, 47, 81, 105
Florida, 31, 77
Foner, Eric, 7, 42, 98, 115, 128
Fort Sumter, 14, 17–18
Fortress Monroe (Virginia), 23
Fourteenth Amendment, 116, 144
Fredericksburg (battle), 41
Freedman's Bank, 126
Freedmen's Bureau. *See* Bureau of Refugees, Freedmen, and Abandoned Lands
free labor (wartime), 69–70, 99–101, 124, 146
free-labor ideology (northern), 9–10, 101, 146–47
Free State Organization (Louisiana), 51–53, 63–65, 80, 105, 124
Frémont, John C., 23–24, 31, 83, 103, 115
fugitive slaves, 23, 26, 30, 35

Georgia, 31, 104, 118
Gettysburg (battle), 45, 57, 89
Gettysburg Address, 57, 60–61, 127–28
Gilmore, James R., 57–58
Grant, Ulysses S., 28, 46, 76, 83, 111, 117, 129–31, 133, 135, 141–42
Greeley, Horace, 33, 54, 90

Hahn, Michael, 36, 47, 80–82, 105–6, 124
Hampton Roads conference, 110, 116–20, 132
Harris, William C., 77
Hay, John, 13, 77, 90, 121
Holzer, Harold, 16
Hood, John Bell, 111, 122
Hooker, Joseph E., 46
Hunter, David, 30–33
Hunter, Robert M. T., 117
Hurlbut, Stephan A., 61–62, 105–6

inaugural address, of Lincoln: first (1861), 16–17; second (1865), 127–28
ironclad oath, 71–72, 84

Jackson, Andrew, 2, 112
Johnson, Andrew, 56, 126: as military governor, 29, 50–51, 61, 78, 106–8, 122–23; as president, 130, 143–45, 147; as vice president, 106, 122–23, 142
Johnston, Joseph E., 129–31, 135

Kansas-Nebraska Act, 7–10
Kentucky, 22, 24
King, R. Cutler, 124

Lee, Robert E., 34, 46, 111, 129–30, 133–34, 136, 142
Lincoln, Abraham: and abolitionists, 7, 22, 30; and abolition of slavery, 45–46, 53, 61; and abolition of slavery in Washington, DC, 27; and African Americans, 7–12, 24–26, 38, 42–43, 54–61, 63–65, 67–70, 81–82, 96–103, 111, 136–41, 143–47; and

Lincoln, Abraham (*continued*)
annual messages to Congress, 26 (1861), 37–41 (1862), 66–74 (1863), 112–15 (1864); and apprenticeship, 69–70, 100, 140; assassination of, 13, 121, 143; and attorney general's ruling on black citizenship, 41, 97; and black suffrage, 5, 10, 71, 81–82, 98, 111, 121–22, 136–47; and black troops, 56–57, 59, 92, 98; and border states, 16, 22, 26–27, 28, 30; and colonization, 11, 24–27, 34, 37–40, 97; and compensated emancipation, 26–27, 30–32, 34–35, 37–41, 97, 119–20; and Confederacy, 2–3, 12–22, 26, 35–38, 42–43, 48–49, 72–74, 86, 109–10, 113–18, 125, 128, 130–35, 137–38; and confiscation (land), 5, 101–3, 126, 132, 146–47; and confiscation acts, 23, 26 (1861), 33 (1862); and contraband policy, 23; and Dred Scott decision, 10; and emancipation policy, 45, 53–61, 89–96, 98, 114, 118–19, 86–87, 96–103, 110–15, 126–31, 136–47; and free labor (wartime), 99–101, 124, 146; and free-labor ideology (northern), 9–10, 101, 146–47; and Frémont's emancipation order, 23–24, 31; and Gettysburg Address, 57, 60–61, 127–28; and Hampton Roads conference, 110, 116–20; and Hunter's emancipation order, 30–33; and inaugural addresses, 16–17 (first), 127–28 (second); issues Emancipation Proclamation, 28–34; and Kansas-Nebraska Act, 7–10; and "last speech," 5, 136–41; and letter to Charles D. Robinson, 92–94; and letter to Horace Greeley, 33; and letter to James C. Conkling, 58–60; and letter to rally at Buffalo, 95–96; and letter to workingmen of Manchester, England, 55; and Lincoln-Douglas debates, 10–11; and meeting with black delegation at White House, 33; and meeting at City Point, Virginia, 129–30; and meeting with John A. Campbell, 131–36; and memorandum to cabinet (1864), 95; and message to Congress on colonization (1862), 26–27; and message to special session of Congress (1861), 17–18, 20–22, 55; and military governors, 29, 36, 88, 141–42; and negotiations with Confederacy, 6, 18, 44–46, 54, 57–58, 60, 89–96, 107,110, 116–20; and postwar reconstruction, 101–3, 128, 143–47; and preliminary emancipation proclamation, 34–37; and proclamation in response to Fort Sumter, 17–18; and Proclamation of Amnesty and Reconstruction, 46, 65–74; and race, 7–12, 24–26, 38, 42–43, 54–61, 67–70, 96–103, 111, 136–41, 143–47; and Radical Republicans, 6–7, 22–23, 30, 70, 77, 81–82, 112, 125–27, 139; and reconstruction, 3–6, 12–15, 17–21, 25, 27, 28–34, 37–43, 48–50, 54, 61, 66–74; and reelection, 13, 103, 108; and secession, 2–3, 12–13, 15–21, 29, 32, 35, 45, 49–50, 70–71, 73, 117–18, 130–31, 137–38; and scholarship on, 1–4, 7–13, 43, 127; and slaveholders, 10, 17, 30, 32–33, 35, 39, 41–42, 64, 74, 96–97, 101, 119–20; and slavery, 7–12, 39, 41, 96–103, 128, 146; and ten-percent plan, 46, 66, 75, 77, 79, 81, 83–87, 89, 100, 104, 106–8, 114, 121–22, 137; and Thirteenth Amendment, 97–98, 115–19; and "To whom it may concern" letter, 90–92; and Union war coalition, 22, 28–34; and Unionists (southern), 15–16, 20–21, 28–30, 35–36, 41, 49, 70–74; and Wade-Davis bill, 87–88; and War Democrats, 22, 28, 30, 44, 77, 91–92, 94–95, 103; and war strategy, 22, 26–28, 113–14, 129–31; and West Virginia, 48–50

Lincoln-Douglas debates, 10–11

Louisiana: abolition of slavery in, 82–83, 103; Emancipation Proclamation in, 37, 42; reconstruction in, 36, 51–53, 63–66, 79–84, 88, 105–6, 123–25, 136–42; Unionists in, 30, 51–53

Maryland, 22, 103

McClellan, George B., 28, 103, 106

McKitrick, Eric, 127

McPherson, James M., 22

Meade, George Gordon, 46

Memphis, 28–29

military governors, 29, 36, 88, 141–42

Mills, Joseph T., 93

Mississippi, 28

Missouri, 22–24, 62–63

Missouri Compromise, 7

Murphy, Isaac, 104–5

Napoleon III, 54

National Equal Rights League, 124–25

negotiations, with Confederacy, 6, 18, 44–46, 54, 57–58, 60, 89–96, 107, 110, 116–20

New Orleans, 29–30, 51–53

New York City draft riots, 60

Nicolay, John G., 95

North Carolina, 20–21, 36, 42, 47–48, 57–58, 77, 130, 141

Oakes, James, 97, 99

Peninsular campaign, 28

Pierpont, Francis Harrison, 21, 48–50, 77

Porter, David, 130

Port Hudson, 53

presidential election, of 1864, 103, 108

Proclamation of Amnesty and Reconstruction, 46, 65–74. *See also* ten-percent plan

race, and Lincoln, 7–12, 24–26, 38, 42–43, 54–61, 67–70, 96–103, 111, 136–41, 143–47. *See also* African Americans; black suffrage

Radical Republicans: and Lincoln, 6–7, 22–23, 30, 70, 77, 81–82, 112, 125–27, 139; and reconstruction policy, 19–20, 47, 72–73, 82–89, 125–27. *See also* Congress; Congressional Republicans

Randall, Alexander W., 93

Raymond, Henry J., 94–95

reconstruction: and Congress, 19–20, 29, 36–37, 47, 83–89, 112, 120–22; and Lincoln, 3–6, 12–15, 17–21, 25, 27, 34, 37–43, 48–50, 54, 61, 66–74, 86–87, 96–103, 126–31, 136–47; postwar, 101–3, 126, 143–47. *See also* Civil War; Confederate States of America; secession

Red River campaign, 79, 81–83

Republican Party, 9, 32, 47, 73, 84–85, 89–91, 94–95, 103, 112, 120–22, 127, 134, 143–45

Robinson, Charles D., 91–94

Rosecrans, Williams S., 46

Sebastian, William K., 61–62

secession: and Lincoln, 2–3, 12–13, 15–21, 29, 32, 35, 45, 49–50, 70–71, 73, 117–18, 130–31, 137–38; and Radical Republicans, 19–20. *See also* Civil War; Confederate States of America; reconstruction

Seward, Frederick, 141

Seward, William H., 41, 53, 112, 116–18, 129, 141

Shenandoah Valley, 103

Shepley, George F., 51–52, 63–65

Sheridan, Philip, 103

Sherman, William T., 76, 83, 103–4, 111, 128–31, 135

Shiloh (Battle), 28

slaveholders, 21, 23–24, 52, 116: and Lincoln, 10, 17, 30, 32–33, 35, 39, 41–42, 64, 74, 96–97, 101, 119–20

slavery, and Lincoln, 7–12, 39, 41, 96–103, 128, 146

Smith, Charles, 124

Snow, William M., 122

South Carolina, 14, 21, 31, 42, 49, 133
Stanton, Edwin M., 29, 64, 112, 141
Steele, Frederick, 78–79, 104–5
Stephens, Alexander H. 43, 117–19
Sumner, Charles, 121, 125, 127

Taney, Roger B., 103
ten-percent plan, 46, 66, 75, 77, 79, 81, 83–87, 89, 100, 104, 106–8, 114, 121–22, 137. *See also* Proclamation of Amnesty and Reconstruction
Tennessee: abolition of slavery in, 123; Emancipation Proclamation in, 37, 42; reconstruction in, 36, 47, 50–51, 61, 78, 106–8, 122–23; Unionists in, 20–21, 28–29, 46, 48, 50–51, 106–8
Thirteenth Amendment, 74, 76, 84, 87, 91, 93, 97–98, 100, 110, 112, 115–19, 124, 133, 138

Unionists (southern), 6, 48–49, 77, 87, 138–39: and abolition of slavery, 45–46; and Lincoln, 15–16, 20–21, 28–30, 35–36, 41, 49, 70–74

Vallandigham, Clement, 54
Vance, Zebulon B., 57–58
Vicksburg (campaign), 45–46, 53, 57, 89
Virginia: abolition of slavery in, 77–78, 104; Emancipation Proclamation in, 36–37, 42; fugitive slaves in, 23; proposed withdrawal from Confederacy, 131–36; Restored Government of, 21, 48–50, 77–78, 133, 141; secession in, 20–21
Vorenberg, Michael, 71

Wade, Benjamin F., 83
Wade-Davis bill, 75–76, 79, 83–89, 120–21
Wade-Davis manifesto, 88–89
War Democrats, 22, 28, 30, 44–45, 91–95
Weitzel, Godfrey, 132–35
Welles, Gideon, 112, 134, 141
Wells, J. Madison, 124
West Virginia, 20–21, 37, 41, 48–50, 133
Whig Party, 7, 9
Wright, Augustus R., 104

John C. Rodrigue is the Lawrence and Theresa Salameno Professor in history at Stonehill College in Easton, Massachusetts. He is the author of several books and other scholarly works, including *Reconstruction in the Cane Fields: From Slavery to Free Labor in Louisiana's Sugar Parishes, 1862–1880*.

CONCISE
LINCOLN
LIBRARY

This series of concise books fills a need for short studies of the life, times, and legacy of President Abraham Lincoln. Each book gives readers the opportunity to quickly achieve basic knowledge of a Lincoln-related topic. These books bring fresh perspectives to well-known topics, investigate previously overlooked subjects, and explore in greater depth topics that have not yet received book-length treatment. For a complete list of titles, see www.conciselincolnlibrary.com.

Other Books in the Concise Lincoln Library

Abraham Lincoln and Horace Greeley
Gregory A. Borchard

Lincoln and the Civil War
Michael Burlingame

Lincoln's Sense of Humor
Richard Carwardine

Lincoln and the Constitution
Brian R. Dirck

Lincoln in Indiana
Brian R. Dirck

Lincoln the Inventor
Jason Emerson

Lincoln and Native Americans
Michael S. Green

Lincoln and the Election of 1860
Michael S. Green

Lincoln and Congress
William C. Harris

Lincoln and the Union Governors
William C. Harris

Lincoln and the Abolitionists
Stanley Harrold

Lincoln's Campaign Biographies
Thomas A. Horrocks

Lincoln in the Illinois Legislature
Ron J. Keller

Lincoln and the Military
John F. Marszalek

Lincoln and Emancipation
Edna Greene Medford

Lincoln and the American Founding
Lucas E. Morel

Lincoln and the Thirteenth Amendment
Christian G. Samito

Lincoln and Medicine
Glenna R. Schroeder-Lein

Lincoln and the Immigrant
Jason H. Silverman

Lincoln and the U.S. Colored Troops
John David Smith

Lincoln's Assassination
Edward Steers, Jr.

Lincoln and Citizenship
Mark E. Steiner

Lincoln and Race
Richard Striner

Lincoln and Religion
Ferenc Morton Szasz with Margaret Connell Szasz

Lincoln and the Natural Environment
James Tackach

Lincoln and the War's End
John C. Waugh

Lincoln as Hero
Frank J. Williams

Abraham and Mary Lincoln
Kenneth J. Winkle